USMARC *Specifications*
for Record Structure, Character Sets, and Exchange Media

Network Development and MARC Standards Office
Library of Congress ■ 1994

USMARC SPECIFICATIONS FOR
Record Structure, Character Sets, and Exchange Media

1994 Edition

Prepared by
Network Development and
MARC Standards Office

Cataloging Distribution Service
Library of Congress ■ Washington

Library of Congress Cataloging-in-Publication Data

USMARC specifications for record structure, character sets,
   and exchange media / prepared by Network Development and
   MARC Standards Office. − 1994 ed.

   Running title: USMARC specifications.
   Includes bibliographical references (p. v).
   ISBN 0-8444-0746-1 (pbk.)
-----Copy 3 Z663.12 .U76   1994
      1. MARC formats−United States. 2. Character sets (Data
processing)−United States. 3. Exchange of bibliographic information
−Data processing−United States. 4. Data tapes. 5. Magnetic disks.
6. Computer files. I. Library of Congress. Network Development and
MARC Standards Office. II. Title: USMARC specifications.
Z699.35.M28U85 1994
025.3'16−dc20   94-041522
                                                                   CIP

Previous (1990) edition published under the title:
USMARC Specifications for Record Structure, Character Sets, Tapes

For sale by the Cataloging Distribution Service, Library of Congress,
Washington, D.C. 20541-5017

This publication will be reissued from time to time as needed to incorporate revisions.

CONTENTS

Contents

INTRODUCTION

GENERAL INFORMATION

USMARC Specifications for Record Structure, Character Sets, and Exchange Media describes the structure of USMARC records, the character sets used in USMARC records, and the formatting of records for exchange on magnetic tape, diskettes, or via electronic file transfer. This document provides technical information on these topics and is intended for the use of personnel involved in the design and maintenance of systems for the exchange and processing of USMARC records.

CHANGES IN 1994 EDITION

The section on record structure reflects the addition of new formats to the USMARC family. The section on character sets contains new Basic and Extended sets for the Arabic script. The section on exchange media has also been expanded considerably to include specifications on the use of magnetic diskettes and electronic file transfer.

STANDARDS AND OTHER RELATED DOCUMENTS

National and international standards:
> *Information Interchange Format* (ANSI Z39.2-1994)
> *Code for Information Interchange* (ASCII) (ANSI X3.4)
> *Code Extension Techniques for Use with 7-bit and 8-bit Character Sets* (ANSI X3.41)
> *Extended Latin Alphabet Coded Character Set for Bibliographic Use* (ANSEL) (ANSI Z39.47)
> *Extension of the Cyrillic Alphabet Coded Character Set for Bibliographic Interchange* (ISO 5427)
> *Format for Bibliographic Information Interchange on Magnetic Tape* (ISO 2709)
> *Greek Alphabet Coded Character Set for Bibliographic Information Interchange* (ISO 5428)
> *Magnetic Tape Labels and File Structure for Information Interchange* (ANSI X3.27-1987)
> *Recorded Magnetic Tape for Information Interchange (800) CPI,NRZI) (ANSI X3.22)*
> *Recorded Magnetic Tape for Information Interchange* (1600 CPI) (ANSI X3.39)
> *Recorded Magnetic Tape for Information Interchange* (6250 CPI, Group-Coded Recording) (ASNI X3.54)

USMARC standards:
> *USMARC Concise Formats*
> *USMARC Format for Authority Data*
> *USMARC Format for Bibliographic Data*
> *USMARC Format for Classification Data*
> *USMARC Format for Community Information*
> *USMARC Format for Holdings Data*
> *USMARC Code List for Languages*
> *USMARC Code List for Countries*
> *USMARC Code List for Geographic Areas*
> *USMARC Code List for Organizations* (formerly, *Symbols of American Libraries*)
> *USMARC Code List for Relators, Sources, Descriptive Conventions*

Other related publications:
> *International Register of Coded Character Sets to be Used with Escape Sequences*, Registration Number 37, Basic Cyrillic Graphic Character Set
> *The USMARC Formats: Background and Principles*

RECORD STRUCTURE

RELATION TO ANSI STANDARD

USMARC is an implementation of the American national standard, *Information Interchange Format* (ANSI Z39.2). This standard specifies the requirements for a generalized interchange format that will accommodate data describing all forms of materials susceptible to bibliographic decription, as well as related information such as authority, classification, community information, and holdings data. The standard presents a generalized structure for records, but does not specify the content of the record and does not, in general, assign meaning to tags, indicators, or data element identifiers. Specification of these elements are provided by particular implementations of the standard. The following description of the USMARC record structure follows the outline of ANSI Z39.2 and indicates the specific choices made for the USMARC implementation of the standard.

DEFINITIONS

Italicized terms within definitions are terms for which definitions are also provided.

base address of data. A *data element* in the *leader* which specifies the first character position of the first *variable field* in the *record* and is equal to the sum of the *lengths* of the leader and the *directory*, including the *field terminator* at the end of the directory.

bibliographic level. A *data element* in the *leader* of bibliographic records which provides additional information about the characteristics and components of the *record*, and is used in conjunction with the *type of record* data element of the leader.

blank (SP). ASCII character 20_{16} (represented graphically in USMARC documentation as b̸), which is used in *indicators* and data elements containing coded values. Generally, blank stands for "undefined," but in some instances it has been assigned a meaning. Also referred to as the space character.

content designation. The codes and conventions established explicitly by USMARC to identify and further characterize the data elements within a *record* and to support the manipulation of that data.

control field. A *variable field* containing information useful or required for the processing of the *record*. Control fields are assigned *tags* beginning with two zeroes.

control number. An ASCII graphic character string uniquely associated with a *record* by the organization transmitting the record and located in a specific *variable field*.

data element. A defined unit of information.

data element identifier. A one-character code used to identify individual data elements within a *variable field*.

data field. A *variable field* containing bibliographic or other data. Data fields are assigned *tags* beginning with characters other than two zeroes.

delimiter. ASCII character $1F_{16}$ (represented graphically in USMARC documentation as ‡), which is combined with a *data element identifier* to make up the *subfield code* which precedes each individual *data element* within a *variable field*. The ASCII name for the delimiter is "unit separator" (US).

directory. An index to the location of the *variable fields* (control and data) within a *record*. The directory consists of *entries*.

encoding level. A *data element* in the *leader* of authority, bibliographic, classification, and holdings records which provides information about the fullness of the information and/or content designation in the *record*.

entry. A *field* within the *directory* which gives the *tag, length* and *starting character position* of a *variable field*.

entry map. A data element in the *leader* which specifies the structure of the *entries* in the *directory*. Always set to 4500 in USMARC records.

field. A defined character string that may contain one or more *data elements*.

field terminator (FT). ASCII character $1E_{16}$, which is used to terminate the *directory* and each *variable field* within a *record*. ASCII name for the field terminator is "record separator" (RS).

fill character. ASCII character $7C_{16}$ (represented graphically in USMARC documentation as |), which has the meaning "no attempt has been made to code".

fixed field. A *field* whose length does not vary. The term is occasionally used to refer to variable *control fields*, especially those that contain coded data such as fields 007 or 008.

identifier length *see* **subfield code count**

indicator. A *data element* associated with a *data field* that supplies additional information about the field. USMARC has reserves two indicator positions in each data field. Each indicator consists of one character; the two indicators appear as the first data elements in a data field. When specific indicator values have not been defined for an indicator, the position contains a blank (SP). Indicators are not used in *control fields*.

indicator count. A *data element* in the *leader* which contains the number positions reserved for *indicators* in each variable *data field*. The indicator count is always set to 2 in USMARC records.

leader. A *fixed field* that occurs at the beginning of each *record* and provides information for the processing of the record.

length. A measure of the size of a data element, field, or record and is expressed in number of characters.

logical record length. A *data element* in the *leader* which contains the length of the entire *record*, including itself and the *record terminator*.

record. A collection of data elements describing or identifying one or more units treated as one logical entity.

record length *see* **logical record length**

record status. A *data element* in the *leader* which indicates the relation of the *record* to a file (e.g., new, updated, etc.).

record terminator (RT). ASCII character 1D₁₆, which is used as the final character of a *record*, following the *field terminator* of the last *data field*. ASCII name for the record terminator is "group separator" (GS).

starting character position. The character position, relative to the *base address of data*, of the first character in the *variable field* referenced by the entry. The first character of the first *field* following the *directory* is numbered 0.

space *see* **blank**

status *see* **record status**

subfield code. The two-character combination of a *delimiter* followed by a *data element identifier*. Subfield codes are not used in *control fields*.

subfield code count. A *data element* in the *leader* which contains the sum of the lengths of the *delimiter* and the *data element identifier* used in the *record*. Always set to 2 in USMARC records.

tag. A three character string used to identify or label an associated *variable field*. The tag may consist of ASCII numeric characters (decimal integers 0-9) and/or ASCII alphabetic characters (uppercase or lowercase, but not both).

type of record. A *data element* in the *leader* which, in conjunction with *bibliographic level*, specifies the characteristics and defines the components of the *record*.

variable control field *see* **control field**

variable data field *see* **data field**

variable field. A *field* whose *length* is determined for each occurrence by the length of data comprising that occurrence. There are two types of variable fields—*control fields* and *data fields*.

CHARACTER SETS

USMARC records are character encoded, including all lengths. In this section on record structure, the data for specified fields are designated as ASCII numeric characters, ASCII lowercase alphabetic characters, ASCII uppercase alphabetic characters, ASCII graphic characters or USMARC characters. The section on character sets defines the repertoire and encoding of these sets of characters.

GENERAL RECORD STRUCTURE

The general structure of a record is represented schematically below.

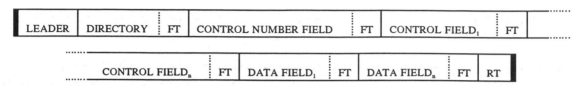

Figure 1: Structure of a USMARC Record

Each record begins with a **leader**, which is a fixed field containing information for the processing of the record. Following the leader is the **directory**, which is an index to the location of the **variable fields** (control and data) within the record. The fields following the directory are all variable fields. The first variable field is the **control number field**, which contains an ASCII graphic character string uniquely associated with the record by the organization transmitting the record. Following the control number field are the rest of the **control fields**, which contain information useful or required for the processing of the record. Following the control fields are **data fields**, which contain general data. A **field terminator** (FT), ASCII character $1E_{16}$, is used to terminate the directory and each variable field within the record. A **record terminator** (RT), ASCII character $1D_{16}$, is used as the final character of the record, following the field terminator of the last data field. These elements of the record are described in more detail in the following sections.

LEADER

The leader is the first field in the record and has a fixed length of 24 characters (character positions 0-23). The structure of the leader as defined in USMARC is represented schematically below. The numbers indicate the character positions occupied by each part of the leader.

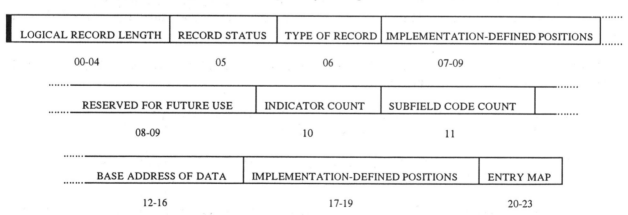

Figure 2: Structure of the Leader in USMARC Records

Logical record length (character positions 00-04), contains a five-character ASCII numeric string equal to the length of the entire record, including itself and the record terminator. The five-character numeric string is right justified and unused positions contain zeroes (zero fill). The maximum length of a record is 99999 characters. ANSI Z39.2 name for this data element is **record length**.

Record status (character position 05), contains an ASCII graphic character which indicates the relation of the record to a file (e.g., new, updated, etc.). ANSI Z39.2 name for this data element is **status**.

Type of record (character position 06), contains an ASCII graphic character which specifies the characteristics and defines the components of the record.

Bibliographic level/Kind of data (character position 07), contains an ASCII graphic character which also provides information about the components and characteristics of the record. It is used in conjunction with the type of record data element. Bibliographic level is not defined in USMARC for authority, classification, or holdings records; in those records character position 07 contains blank (ƀ). In community information records, Leader position 07 is defined for **Kind of data**.

Character positions 08-09 are not defined in in USMARC for bibliographic, authority, or holdings records. These positions contain blanks.

Indicator count (character position 10), contains a single-character ASCII numeric string equal to the number of indicators occurring in each variable data field. In USMARC records, the indicator count is always 2.

Subfield code count (character position 11), contains a single-character ASCII numeric string equal to the sum of the lengths of the delimiter and the data element identifier used in the record. In USMARC records, the subfield code count is always 2. ANSI Z39.2 name for this data element is **identifier length**.

Base address of data (character positions 12-16), contains a five-character ASCII numeric string which specifies the first character position of the first variable field in the record and is equal to the sum of the lengths of the leader and the directory, including the field terminator at the end of the directory. The number is right justified and unused positions contain zeroes (zero fill).

ANSI Z39.2 reserves character positions 17-19 for definition by a particular implementation. The individual USMARC format documents for bibliographic, authority and holdings records define these character positions for each particular type of record.

Entry map (character positions 20-23), contains four single digit ASCII numeric characters which specify the structure of the entries in the directory.

- **Length of length-of-field** (character position 20): specifies the length of that portion of each directory entry; in USMARC records, it is always set to 4.

- **Length of starting-character-position** (character position 21): specifies the length of that portion of each directory entry; in USMARC records, it is always set to 5.

- **Length of implementation-defined** (character position 22): specifies that portion of each directory entry; in USMARC records, a directory entry does not contain an implementation-defined portion, therefore this position is always set to 0.

- **Undefined** (character position 23): this character position in the entry map is undefined; it is always set to 0.

LENGTH OF LENGTH-OF-FIELD	LENGTH OF STARTING-CHARACTER-POSITION	LENGTH OF IMPLEMENTATION-DEFINED	UNDEFINED
20	21	22	23

Figure 3: Structure of an Entry Map in USMARC Record

DIRECTORY

A directory entry in USMARC is made up of a tag, length-of-field, and field starting position. The directory begins in character position 24 of the record and ends with a field terminator. It is of variable length and consists of a series of fixed fields, referred to as "entries." One entry is associated with each variable field (control or data) present in the record. Each directory entry is 12 characters in length; the structure of each entry as defined in USMARC is represented schematically below. The numbers indicate the character positions occupied by the parts of the entry.

TAG	FIELD LENGTH	STARTING CHARACTER POSITION
00-02	03-06	07-11

Figure 4: Structure of a Directory Entry in USMARC Records

Tag (character positions 00-02), consists of three ASCII numeric characters or ASCII alphabetic characters (uppercase or lowercase, but not both) used to identify or label an associated variable field. The USMARC formats have used only numeric tags. The tag is stored only in the directory entry for the field; it does not appear with the variable field itself.

Field length (character positions 03-06), contains four ASCII numeric characters which give the length, expressed as a decimal number, of the variable field to which the entry corresponds. This length includes the indicators, subfield codes, data and field terminator associated with the field. A field length number of fewer than four digits is right justified and unused positions contain zeroes (zero fill). USMARC sets the length of the field-length portion of the entry at four characters, thus a field may contain a maximum of 9999 characters.

Starting character position (character positions 07-11) contains five ASCII numeric characters which give the starting character position, expressed as a decimal number, of the variable field to which the entry corresponds relative to the base address of data of the record. A starting character position of fewer than five digits is right justified and unused positions contain zeroes (zero fill).

Directory entries for control fields precede entries for data fields. Entries for control fields are sequenced by tag in increasing numerical order. Entries for data fields are arranged in ascending order according to the first character of the tag, with numeric characters preceding alphabetic characters.

VARIABLE FIELDS

The variable fields follow the leader and the directory in the record and consist of control fields and data fields. Control fields precede data fields in the record and are arranged in the same sequence as the corresponding entries in the directory. The sequence in which data fields are stored in the record is not necessarily the same as the order of the corresponding directory entries.

Control fields in USMARC formats are assigned tags beginning with two zeroes. They are comprised of data and a field terminator; they do not contain indicators or subfield codes. The control number field is assigned tag 001 and contains the control number of the record. Each record contains only one control number field (with tag 001), which is to be located at the base address of data.

Data fields in USMARC formats are assigned tags beginning with ASCII numeric characters other than two zeroes. Such fields contain indicators and subfield codes, as well as data and a field terminator. There are no restrictions on the number, length, or content of data fields other than those already stated or implied, e.g., those resulting from the limitation of total record length. The structure of a data field is shown schematically below.

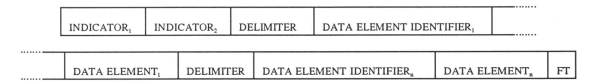

Figure 5: Structure of a Variable Data Field in USMARC Records

The two **indicators** occupy the first character positions of a variable data field, preceding any subfield code (delimiter plus data element identifier) which may be present. Each data field in the record includes two indicators, even if values have not been defined for the indicators in a particular field. Indicators supply additional information about the field, and are defined individually for each field. Indicator values are interpreted independently; meaning is not ascribed to the two indicators taken together. Indicators may be any ASCII lowercase alphabetic or numeric character or the blank (ASCII SPACE). The USMARC formats have used numeric values for indicators. A blank is used in an undefined indicator position or to mean *information not provided* in a defined indicator position. The numeric character 9 is reserved for local definition as an indicator.

Subfield codes identify the individual data elements within the field, and precede the data elements they identify. Each data field contains at least one subfield code. The subfield code consists of a delimiter [$1F_{16}$, 8-bit] followed by a data element identifier. Data element identifiers defined in USMARC may be any ASCII lowercase alphabetic or numeric character. In general, numeric identifiers are defined for data used to process the field, or coded data needed to interpret the field. Alphabetic identifiers are defined for the separate elements which constitute the data content of the field. The character 9 and the following ASCII graphic symbols are reserved for local definition as data element identifiers:

$$! \quad " \quad \# \quad \$ \quad \% \quad \& \quad ' \quad (\quad) \quad * \quad + \quad , \quad - \quad . \quad / \quad : \quad ; \quad < \quad = \quad > \quad ?$$

A data field may contain more than one data element, depending upon the definition of the field. The last character in a data field is the **field terminator**, which follows the last data element in the field.

DESIGN PRINCIPLES FOR USMARC

A USMARC format is a set of codes and content designators defined for encoding a particular type of machine-readable record. The USMARC formats as a group serve as a vehicle for authority, bibliographic, classification, community information, and holdings data of all types. These formats are intended to be communication formats and are primarily designed to provide specifications for the exchange of information between systems. The following description of design principles repeats, in some cases, information given above but is given again for completeness.

Content designation

The purpose of content designation is to identify and characterize the data elements which comprise a USMARC record with sufficient precision to support manipulation of the data for a variety of functions. The USMARC formats have attempted to preserve consistency of content designation across formats where this is appropriate. While these formats are designed for use within the United States, attempts have been made to preserve compatibility of content designation with other national formats.

The USMARC formats support the sorting of data only to a limited extent. In general, sorting must be accomplished through the application of external algorithms to the data.

The USMARC formats provide for using content designation, e.g., tag values or indicators, to specify display constants. A display constant is a term, phrase, and/or spacing or punctuation convention that may be system generated under prescribed circumstances to make a visual presentation of data in a record more meaningful to a user. Such display constants are not carried in the data, but may be supplied for display by the processing system.

Variable fields and tags

The data in a USMARC record is organized into fields, each identified by a three-character tag. Although ANSI Z39.2 allows both alphabetic and numeric characters, USMARC formats use only numeric tags. The tag is stored in the directory entry for the field, not in the field itself. Variable fields are grouped into blocks according to the first character of the tag, which, with some exceptions, identifies the function of the data within a record. The type of information in the field is identified by the remainder of the tag. The meaning of these blocks depends upon the type of record.

The bibliographic format blocks are:

0XX	Control information, numbers, and codes
1XX	Main entry
2XX	Titles and title paragraph (title, edition, imprint)
3XX	Physical description, etc.
4XX	Series statements
5XX	Notes
6XX	Subject access fields
7XX	Added entries other than subject or series; linking fields
8XX	Series added entries, etc.
9XX	Reserved for local implementation

These guidelines apply only to the main range of fields in each block, not to secondary ranges in the bibliographic format such as the linking fields in 760-787 or the variant name fields in 870-873.

The authority format blocks are:

0XX	Control information, numbers, and codes
1XX	Heading
2XX	Complex see references
3XX	Complex see also references
4XX	See from tracings
5XX	See also from tracings
6XX	Reference notes, treatment decisions, notes, etc.
7XX	Not defined
8XX	Not defined
9XX	Reserved for local implementation

The classification format blocks are:

0XX	Control information, numbers, and codes
1XX	Classification numbers and terms
2XX	Complex see references
3XX	Complex see also references
4XX	Invalid number tracings
5XX	Valid number tracings
6XX	Note fields
70X-75X	Index term fields
76X	Number building fields
8XX	Not defined
9XX	Reserved for local implementation

The community information format blocks are:

0XX	Control information, numbers, and codes
1XX	Primary names
2XX	Titles, addresses
3XX	Physical information, etc.
4XX	Series information
5XX	Notes
6XX	Subject access fields
7XX	Added entries other than subject
8XX	Alternate graphics
9XX	Reserved for local implementation

The holdings format blocks are:

0XX	Control information, numbers, and codes
1XX	Not defined
2XX	Not defined
3XX	Not defined
4XX	Not defined
5XX	Notes
6XX	Not defined
7XX	Not defined
8XX	Holdings and location data, notes
9XX	Reserved for local implementation

Within some blocks of variable fields in bibliographic records (1XX, 4XX, 6XX, 7XX, 8XX) and authority records (1XX, 4XX, 5XX), parallels of content designation are preserved. The following meanings are generally given to the final two characters of the tag of fields in these blocks:

X00	Personal names
X10	Corporate names
X11	Meeting names
X30	Uniform titles
X40	Bibliographic titles
X50	Topical terms
X51	Geographic names

Note fields

The USMARC formats prescribe when a separate field should be defined for note data and when the data should be included in a general note field. For the USMARC bibliographic format, a specific 5XX note field is defined when at least one of the following is true:

1) Categorical indexing or retrieval is required on the data defined for the note. The note is used for structured access purposes but does not have the nature of a controlled access point.

2) Special manipulation of that specific category of data is a routine requirement. Such manipulation includes special print or display formatting or selection or suppression from display or printed product.

3) Specialized structuring of information for reasons other than those given above, e.g., to support particular standards of data content when they cannot be supported in existing fields.

For the USMARC authority format, the specifications for notes are covered in the following two conditions:

1) A specific note field is needed when special manipulation of that specific category of data is a routine requirement. Such manipulation includes special print or display formatting or selection or suppression from display or printed product.

2) Multiple notes are generally not established to accommodate the same type of information for different types of authorities. Notes are thus not differentiated by or limited to subject, name, or series if the same information applies to more than one type.

Local fields

Certain tags have been reserved for local implementation. With the exception of the fields noted below, the USMARC formats specify no structure or meaning for local fields. Communication of such fields between systems is governed by mutual agreements on the content and content designation of the fields communicated.

In general, any tag containing the character 9 is reserved for local implementation within the block structure. Specifically the 9XX block is reserved for local implementation as indicated above. The historical development of the USMARC formats has left one exception to this general principle: field 490 (Series Statment) in the bibliographic format. There are several obsolete fields with tags containing the

---

character 9 (e.g., 009 (Physical Description Fixed-Field for Archival Collection) and 039 (Level of Bibliographic Control and Coding Detail)). The indicator value 9 and subfield ǂ9 are reserved for local implementation as well.

Repeatability

Theoretically, all fields, except 001 (Control Number) and 005 (Date and Time of Lastest Transaction), and subfields may be repeated. The nature of the data, however, often precludes repetition (e.g., a bibliographic or community information record may contain only one field 245 (Title Statement); an authority or classification record may contain only one 1XX heading field). The repeatability or nonrepeatability of each field and subfield is specified in the USMARC formats.

Coded data

In addition to content designation, the USMARC formats include specifications for the content of certain data elements, particularly those which provide for the representation of data by coded values. Coded values consist of fixed-length character strings. Individual elements within a coded-data field or subfield are identified by relative character position. Although coded data occur most frequently in the leader, directory, and variable control fields, any field or subfield may be defined for coded data.

Certain common values for codes used in coded data have been defined:

ƀ	Undefined (element not defined)
n	Not applicable (element not applicable to the item)
u	Unknown (record creator was unable to determine value)
z	Other (value other than those defined for the element)
|	Fill character (record creator has chosen not to provide information)

Historical exceptions to these definitions occur in the formats. In particular, the blank (ƀ) has been defined as *not applicable*, or has been assigned a meaning.

CHARACTER SETS

INTRODUCTION

All content designation in USMARC records is encoded using the *Code for Information Interchange* (ASCII) (ANSI X3.4). Other character sets such as the *Extended Latin Alphabet Coded Character Set for Bibliographic Use* (ANSEL) (ANSI Z39.47) and USMARC character codes for 14 superscript characters, 14 subscript characters, and 3 Greek symbols are commonly used in records with Latin script data content. Additional characters sets for the Arabic, Chinese, Cyrillic, Hebrew, Japanese, and Korean scripts have been designated for use in USMARC records. The following describes the use of these character sets. Tables and lists of the USMARC character sets appear beginning on pages 22 of this document.

DEFINITIONS

Italicized terms found within definitions are terms for which definitions are also provided.

bit combination. A sequence of consecutive bits that represents a *character*.

byte. A group of consecutive bits; in current applications the number of bits varies from 7 or 8 to 16 or 32. An 8-bit byte is also called an *octet*.

character. A member of a set of elements used for the organization, control or representation of data.

coded character set; code. A set of unambiguous rules that establish a character set and the one-to-one relationships between the *characters* of the set and their *bit combinations*.

code extension. The techniques for encoding *characters* that are not included in a given *coded character set*.

code table. A table showing the *character* allocated to each *bit combination* in a *coded character set*.

code table position. That part of a *code table* identified by its column and row coordinates.

combining characters (diacritics). A character representing a mark, point, or sign used in conjunction with alphabetic graphic characters to distinguish them in form or sound (usually intended to be displayed above or below an alphabetic graphic character).

control character. A *control function* that is coded as a single *bit combination*.

control function. An action that affects the recording, processing, transmission or interpretation of data and that has a coded representation consisting of one or more *bit combinations*.

designate. To identify a set of *characters* that are to be represented in a prescribed manner.

diacritics (character modifiers). A mark, point, or sign used with an alphabet base letter to distinguish it in form or sound from an unmodified letter.

escape (ESC). A *control character* (ASCII $1B_{16}$) which is used to provide additional *characters* by *code extension*. It alters the meaning of a limited number of contiguously following *bit combinations*.

escape sequence. A bit string that is used for control purposes in *code extension* procedures and that consists of two or more *bit combinations*, of which the first is the bit combination corresponding to the *Escape* character.

field orientation. Refers to the direction that displayed or printed *graphic characters* in a field are intended to be written (e.g., either from left to right, or from right to left). The characters are always recorded in their logical order, from the first character to the last character, irrespective of the direction they are intended to be read.

field orientation code. A code that indicates the direction in which the displayed or printed *graphic characters* are intended to be written.

final character. The *character* whose *bit combination* terminates an *escape sequence*.

graphic character. A *character*, other than a *control character*, that has a visual representation normally handwritten, printed, or displayed.

intermediate character. A *character* whose *bit combination* occurs between the *Escape* character and the *final character* in a *escape sequence* consisting of more than two *bit combinations*.

invoke. To cause a *designated* set of *characters* to be represented by the prescribed *bit combinations* whenever those bit combinations occur.

nonspacing graphic character. A graphic character whose use is not followed by the forward movement of the output device. For the purpose of this standard, the term includes character modifiers.

octet. A group of 8 consecutive bits, also referred to as an 8-bit *byte*.

punctuation mark. A mark that indicates the structure of sentence or phrase for clearness (e.g., ;).

space (SP). ASCII character 20_{16} which is interpreted both as a *graphic character* and as a *control character*. This *character* is also referred to as "blank" (represented graphically as ƀ) in USMARC documentation.

spacing graphic character. A graphic character whose use is followed by the forward movement of the out device to the next character position. For the purpose of this standard, the term includes special characters, special symbols, and punctuation marks.

special character. An alphabetic character or other spacing graphic character (e.g., Æ).

special symbol. A conventional sign used in place of words or word groups (e.g., &).

working set. The *coded character set* currently *invoked*.

IMPLEMENTATION

ASCII as used in USMARC records has been extended to an 8-bit code, thus the basic USMARC code set is 8-bit. The individual characters are commonly referred to by hexadecimal notation. The hex codes for characters may be determined from the code matrix column number and row number. For instance, the SPACE character, which is expressed in binary notation as 0010 0000, is expressed in hexadecimal notation as 20, (also written as 20_{16}).

There are control characters defined in ASCII that are not used in a USMARC communications record (e.g., null, ASCII 00_{16}). There are also spacing graphic characters in ASCII which closely resemble nonspacing combining characters in ANSEL (i.e., spacing circumflex (ASCII $3E_{16}$), spacing underscore (ASCII $5F_{16}$), spacing grave (ASCII 60_{16}), and spacing tilde (ASCII $7E_{16}$)). In USMARC records, the use of the spacing ASCII diacritical marks is limited to the encoding of file names, etc., where the intent is not to represent a letter-with-diacritic combination.

An 8-bit coded character set accommodates two sets of 32 control functions (C0 and C1), two sets of 94 graphic characters (G0 and G1), a SPACE character, a DELETE character, and two reserved character positions. (See *Figure 6*.) C0 and C1 control functions, and the SPACE character can be accessed at anytime as they are not affected by the designation and invocation of different graphic sets.

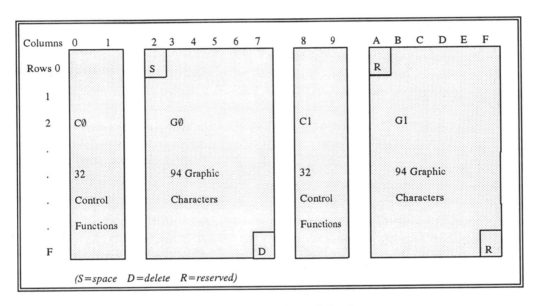

Figure 6: 8-bit Code Matrix

Graphic character sets may be represented by either 8 bits per character, or, where a larger number of characters needs to be accommodated by the character set, by more than 8 bits codes per character (usually in multiples of 8).

According to *Code Extension Techniques for Use with 7-bit and 8-bit Character Sets* (ANSI X3.41), the general technique for the use of code sets requires first the **designation** of the sets, then the **invocation** of a designated set as the **working** set. For 8-bit codes, two sets of control functions and four graphic character sets may be designated at any given time. The designated sets of control functions are called the C0 and C1 sets. The designated sets of graphic characters are called the G0, G1, G2, and G3 sets. Two C_n and two G_n sets may be in an invoked, working set status at any given time. If, for example, a specific character set is designated as the G0 set and invoked as the working set, in order to

---

change a working set either another character set must be designated as the G0 set, or another character set must be designated as set G1, G2 or G3 and that set invoked as a working set. The following sections specify the designation and invocation of code sets in USMARC.

CONTROL FUNCTION SETS

The C0 and C1 control function sets are fixed for USMARC. They are thus designated and invoked by default and need not be designated and invoked in the record.

The C0 set is the set of 32 control functions defined in ASCII. They occupy codes 00_{16} through $1F_{16}$ at all times. This set contains the basic control characters, of which only four characters may be used in USMARC records. These four characters are the escape character ($1B_{16}$), subfield delimiter ($1F_{16}$), field terminator ($1E_{16}$), and record terminator ($1D_{16}$).

The C1 set is another set of 32 possible control characters which occupy codes 80_{16} through $9F_{16}$ at all times. There are two control character currently defined for use in USMARC records. They are the joiner $8D_{16}$ and nonjoiner $8E_{16}$. These characters are used to control the environment of characters whose proximity to other characters affects their processing.

GRAPHIC CHARACTER SETS

ASCII graphics are the designated G0 set and ANSEL graphics are the designated G1 set for USMARC records. ASCII graphics are invoked as the working set for codes 21_{16} through $7E_{16}$. ANSEL, a graphic character set of nonspacing and spacing marks and special signs, is designated as the graphic G1 set, invoked as the working set for codes $A1_{16}$ through FE_{16}. These are the default working sets. ASCII and ANSEL are used for data transcribed within fields and subfields, but alternate graphic character sets may also be accessed using special techniques. Upon exit from a subfield, ASCII must be designated the G0 set and ANSEL the G1 set.

There are two special characters positions in every "G" code block (e.g., G0) assigned to graphic characters; one at the beginning (20_{16} or $A0_{16}$ in an 8-bit environment) and one at the end ($7F_{16}$ or FF_{16} in an 8-bit environment). The *space* character, which is interpreted both as a *graphic character* and as a *control character*, occupies the first of these two special character positions. In USMARC records it is used in indicators, coded data elements, and variable fields. This *character* is also referred to as "blank" (represented graphically as ƀ) in USMARC documentation. The *delete* character occupies the second of the two special character positions. It is a *control character* that is not used in USMARC records.

NONSPACING GRAPHIC CHARACTERS (DIACRITICS)

Nonspacing graphic characters are always used in conjunction with other spacing graphic characters. More than one nonspacing graphic character may be associated with one spacing graphic character. USMARC does not use the ASCII spacing equivalents of the ANSEL nonspacing graphic characters to encode diacritical marks associated with alphabetic characters. The nonspacing graphic characters that are used in conjunction with ASCII spacing graphic characters appear in the ANSEL character set in columns E-F (8-bit, G1 set). In the Arabic character set, nonspacing characters appear in columns 4-7, and F (8-bit set). In the Hebrew character set, nonspacing characters appear in column 4 (8-bit, G0 set). In a character string, these nonspacing characters precede the character that they modify. When a graphic character requires multiple character modifiers, they are entered in the order in which they appear, reading left to right (or right to left with right-to-left scripts) and top to bottom.

ACCESSING ALTERNATE GRAPHIC CHARACTER SETS

There are currently two techniques established in USMARC to access an alternate graphic character set. One way is a special technique for accessing a small number of characters; the other involves using standard escape sequences to access any well defined character set. Below is an explanation of these two techniques.

Technique 1: Greek Symbols, Subscript, and Superscript Characters

Three Greek symbols (alpha, beta, and gamma), fourteen subscript characters, and fourteen superscript characters have been placed in three separate character sets that are accessed by a locking escape sequence. The technique for accessing these characters is outside the framework specified in ANSI X3.41. These three special sets are designated as G0 sets in codes 21_{16} through $7E_{16}$ by means of a two-character sequence consisting of the *Escape* character and an ASCII *graphic character*. The specific escape sequences for the three special sets are:

ESCg (ASCII $1B_{16}$ 67_{16}) for the Greek symbol set

ESCb (ASCII $1B_{16}$ 62_{16}) for the Subscript set

ESCp (ASCII $1B_{16}$ 70_{16}) for the Superscript set

When one of these character sets is designated using the escape sequence, the escape is locking which means that all characters following the escape sequence are interpreted as being part of the newly designated character set until another escape sequence is encountered. This follow-on escape sequence may redesignate ASCII or designate another special character set as the G0 set. To redesignate ASCII, the following two-character escape sequence is used:

ESCs (ASCII $1B_{16}$ 73_{16}) for ASCII default character set

See pages 26-29 for code tables and listings of these three character sets.

Technique 2: Other Alternate Graphic Character Sets

All other alternate graphic character sets should be designated and invoked in accordance with ANSI X3.41, *Code Extension Techniques for Use with 7-bit and 8-bit Character Sets*. At the present time, additional sets are accessed through designation as either G0 (codes 21_{16} through $7E_{16}$) or G1 (codes $A1_{16}$ through FE_{16}). At some time in the future, if required, more extensive designation and invocation as specified in ANSI X3.41 may be allowed in USMARC.

Alternate graphic character sets are designated by means of a multiple character escape sequence consisting of the ESCAPE character, an Intermediate character sequence, and a Final character sequence in the form ESC I F, where:

■ ESC is the ESCAPE character (ASCII $1B_{16}$).

■ I is the Intermediate character sequence, which may be one or more characters in length and indicates whether the set is designated as the G0 set or the G1 set and whether the set has one byte or multiple bytes per character.

The following values may be used for the Intermediate character sequence:

To designate as the G0 set:
   For a set with one byte per character
      $I = 28_{16}$ [ASCII graphic: ( ]
   or $I = 2C_{16}$ [ASCII graphic: ,].

   For a set with multiple bytes per character
      $I = 24_{16}$ [ASCII graphic: $]
   or $I = 24_{16}\ 2C_{16}$ [ASCII graphics: $,].

To designate as the G1 set:
   For a set with one byte per character
      $I = 29_{16}$ [ASCII graphic:)]
   or $I = 2D_{16}$ [ASCII graphic: -].

   For a set with multiple bytes per character
      $I = 24_{16}\ 29_{16}$ [ASCII graphics: $)]
   or $I = 24_{16}\ 2D_{16}$ [ASCII graphics: $ -].

■ F is the Final character in the escape sequence, which identifies the graphic character set being designated. The codes for Final characters are assigned by the registration authority of the International Organization for Standardization (ISO) for many sets. These sets are assigned codes in the range 40_{16} through $7E_{16}$; other character sets intended for local use may be assigned a code outside this range. The Final characters for alternate graphic character sets approved for use in USMARC are the following:

33_{16} [ASCII graphic: 3] = Basic Arabic

34_{16} [ASCII graphic: 4] = Extended Arabic

42_{16} [ASCII graphic: B] = ASCII

--   [not yet assigned] = ANSEL

31_{16} [ASCII graphic: 1] = Chinese, Japanese, Korean (EACC)

$4E_{16}$ [ASCII graphic: N] = Basic Cyrillic

51_{16} [ASCII graphic: Q] = Extended Cyrillic

53_{16} [ASCII graphic: S] = Greek symbols

32_{16} [ASCII graphic: 2] = Basic Hebrew

Whenever alternate graphic character sets accessed using Technique 2 are used in a USMARC bibliographic record, field 066 (Character Sets Present) must appear in the record. The alternate graphic character sets are identified in subfield ǂc of field 066 to assist machine processing. Field 880 (Alternate Graphic Representation) will appear in the record to carry the data in the indicated alternate graphic character set. [See *USMARC Format for Bibliographic Data*, fields 066 and 880]

Use and Placement of Escape Sequences

Escape sequences to designate alternate graphic character sets may occur wherever the alternate characters are needed, e.g., within a word, at the beginning of a subfield, or in the middle of a subfield. However, the escape sequence never replaces a space.

Escape sequences are locking. The alternate graphic character set remains designated as the G_n set until another graphic character set is designated. If the ASCII graphics have been displaced as the G0 set within a subfield, ASCII graphics must be designated as the G0 set before subfield delimiters and field terminators. Some alternate character sets include separately defined marks of punctuation that duplicate those defined in ASCII. They may be used when the alternate graphics are used.

Example: **880 10 ‡ 6245-02/(N ‡ aE(NOхрана природной среды/E(B ‡ cE(NЮ.И. Подлипского.E(B**

NOTE: The escape sequences follow Technique 2, where
  E = ESCAPE character
  (= set is to be designated as the G0 set and has one byte per character
  N = ISO Basic Cyrillic character set
  B = ASCII default character set

When the text of a field which has an indicator for nonfiling characters begins with an escape sequence, the bytes in the escape sequence are not included in the count of nonfiling characters.

FIELD ORIENTATION

The contents of a field in a USMARC record are always recorded in their logical order, from the first character to the last, regardless of *field orientation*. For example, the *graphic character* for the first letter of a title in Hebrew (which would be read from right to left) follows immediately after the subfield pair which begins the field and the escape sequence which invokes the alternate character set for the basic Hebrew alphabet. The first character of the title does not occur at the end of the field just before the field terminator.

Example: **880 10 ‡ 6260-04/(2/r ‡ aE(2תל ביבא :E(B ‡ bE(2משרד הבטחון,E(B ‡ c1989E(2.E(B**
  [Order of data in USMARC record]

Example: תל אביב : משרד הבטחון, 1989.
  [Order of data as it might be displayed, with Hebrew script starting from the right]

NOTE: The escape sequences follow Technique 2, where
  E = ESCAPE character
  (= set is to be designated as the G0 set and has one byte per character
  2 = Hebrew character set
  B = ASCII default character set

Left-to-right *field orientation* is the default for fields in USMARC records. No special designation of field orientation is required for character sets with left-to-right orientation. When a field contains data whose orientation is from right to left, orientation is indicated with a field orientation code appended to subfield ‡6 (Linkage). [See *USMARC Format for Bibliographic Data*, field 880.]

The decision to designate the field orientation as right-to-left depends on the predominance of data in a script that is read right-to-left at the field and/or the record level. A field may contain a mixture of scripts. Right-to-left field orientation is usually designated in the following instances:

- when a field contains only or mostly data in a right-to-left script

- when a field contains data in both a right-to-left and a left-to-right script, but the preponderance of data in other fields is right-to-left

- in order to maintain consistency among fields constituting the "body" of a bibliographic entry (2XX, 3XX, and 4XX fields)

FILL CHARACTER

The key to retaining the MARC structure, while simultaneously reducing required coding specificity, is the fill character. For USMARC records, the use of this fill character is limited to variable control fields such as field 008 (Fixed-Length Data Elements). It may not be used in the leader or in tags, indicators, or subfield codes. Presence of a fill character in a variable control field indicates that the creator of the record has not attempted to supply a value. In contrast, use of a code value for "unknown" in a variable control field indicates that the creator of the record has attempted to supply a value, but was unable to determine what the appropriate value should be. The fill character may be used in undefined character positions and in character positions for which the USMARC format defines one or more values. Use of the fill character in variable control fields is usually regulated by the policy of the inputting agency.

For communication purposes, the fill character is represented by the code $7C_{16}$ in the expanded 8-bit ASCII character set. The fill character is represented graphically as the vertical bar (|).

CHARACTER SET SUBSETS

In USMARC documents, character set subsets are specified by the following names with the definition indicated:

ASCII numerics:	Graphic repertoire and encoding found in ASCII positions 30_{16} through 39_{16}.
ASCII uppercase alphabetics:	Graphic repertoire and encoding found in ASCII positions 41_{16} through $4F_{16}$ and 50_{16} through $5A_{16}$.
ASCII lowercase alphabetics:	Graphic repertoire and encoding found in ASCII positions 61_{16} through $6F_{16}$ and 70_{16} through $7A_{16}$.
ASCII graphic symbols:	Graphic repertoire and encoding found in ASCII positions 20_{16} through $2F_{16}$, $3A_{16}$ through $3F_{16}$, 40_{16}, $5B_{16}$ through $5F_{16}$, 60_{16}, and $7B_{16}$ through $7E_{16}$, which includes all ASCII characters other than numerics, alphabetics and delete.
ASCII graphics:	All ASCII characters (including numerics, alphabetics and graphic symbols) found in positions 20_{16} through $7E_{16}$.

USMARC: All characters defined in this document and other character set
                                           documentation specified for use in USMARC.

CODE TABLES AND LISTS

The following sections contain code tables and code lists for the 8-bit ASCII and ANSEL character sets, special Greek symbols, subscript, and superscript character sets (accessed using Technique 1 above), and character sets for several other scripts. Because of its size and complexity, the character set for Chinese, Japanese, and Korean, is not given here. It is published separately as ANSI/NISO Z39.64, *East Asian Character Code for Bibliographic Use*. In all tables and lists, only those characters which may be used in USMARC records are specified with their appropriate code values. All codes not used are reserved for future definition in USMARC.

Table 1: Basic Latin (ASCII) and Extended Latin (ANSEL) Character Sets (8-bit)

Bits 8,7→		00				01				10				11			
Bits 6,5→		00	01	10	11	00	01	10	11	00	01	10	11	00	01	10	11
Hex 1→		0	1	2	3	4	5	6	7	8	9	A	B	C	D	E	F
00 00	0	///	///	SP	0	@	P	`✠	p	///	///	■	'	º	▩	ʾ	ˎ
01	1	///	///	!	1	A	Q	a	q	///	///	Ł	ł	ℓ	▩	`	ˌ
10	2	///	///	"	2	B	R	b	r	///	///	Ø	ø	℗	▩	´	.
11	3	///	///	#	3	C	S	c	s	///	///	Đ	đ	©	▩	^	..
01 00	4	///	///	$	4	D	T	d	t	///	///	Þ	þ	♯	▩	~	°
01	5	///	///	%	5	E	U	e	u	///	///	Æ	æ	¿	▩	¯	=
10	6	///	///	&	6	F	V	f	v	///	///	Œ	œ	¡	▩	˘	_
11	7	///	///	'	7	G	W	g	w	///	///	ʹ	″	▩	▩	˙	ˌ
10 00	8	///	///	(	8	H	X	h	x	///	///	·	ı	▩	▩	¨	¸
01	9	///	///	)	9	I	Y	i	y	///	///	♭	£	▩	▩	ˇ	˳
10	A	///	///	*	:	J	Z	j	z	///	///	®	ð	▩	▩	°	⁀
11	B	///	ESC	+	;	K	[	k	{	///	///	±	▩	▩	▩	⁀	⁔
11 00	C	///	///	,	<	L	\	l	|	///	///	Ơ	ơ	▩	▩	⁀	▩
01	D	///	GS	-	=	M	]	m	}	JNR	///	Ư	ư	▩	▩	'	▩
10	E	///	RS	.	>	N	^✠	n	~✠	NJR	///	ʼ	▩	▩	▩	″	'
11	F	///	US	/	?	O	_✠	o	■	///	///	▩	▩	▩	▩	˘	■

↑ ↑ ↑	⎣___⎦ C0 (ASCII)	⎣___⎦ G0 (ASCII)	⎣___⎦ C1	⎣___⎦ G1 (ANSEL)
4,3 2,1 0 Bits Hex	↑	↑	↑	↑

✠ Spacing Latin character, not to be confused with similar nonspacing Latin character

/// Reserved for control characters

▩ Reserved for future standardization

■ Corners (reserved)

Code List for the Basic Latin (ASCII) and Extended Latin (ANSEL) Character Sets (8-bit)

Hex	Binary	Graphic	Name/Function	Hex	Binary	Graphic	Name/Function
00	0000 0000		[RESERVED]	2F	0010 1111	/	SLASH
01	0000 0001		[RESERVED]	30	0011 0000	0	
02	0000 0010		[RESERVED]	31	0011 0001	1	
03	0000 0011		[RESERVED]	32	0011 0010	2	
04	0000 0100		[RESERVED]	33	0011 0011	3	
05	0000 0101		[RESERVED]	34	0011 0100	4	
06	0000 0110		[RESERVED]	35	0011 0101	5	
07	0000 0111		[RESERVED]	36	0011 0110	6	
08	0000 1000		[RESERVED]	37	0011 0111	7	
09	0000 1001		[RESERVED]	38	0011 1000	8	
0A	0000 1010		[RESERVED]	39	0011 1001	9	
0B	0000 1011		[RESERVED]	3A	0011 1010	:	COLON
0C	0000 1100		[RESERVED]	3B	0011 1011	;	SEMICOLON
0D	0000 1101		[RESERVED]	3C	0011 1100	<	LESS-THAN SIGN
0E	0000 1110		[RESERVED]				(OPENING ANGLE BRACKET)
0F	0000 1111		[RESERVED]	3D	0011 1101	=	EQUALS SIGN
10	0001 0000		[RESERVED]	3E	0011 1110	>	GREATER-THAN SIGN
11	0001 0001		[RESERVED]				(CLOSING ANGLE BRACKET)
12	0001 0010		[RESERVED]	3F	0011 1111	?	QUESTION MARK
13	0001 0011		[RESERVED]	40	0100 0000	@	COMMERCIAL AT
14	0001 0100		[RESERVED]	41	0100 0001	A	
15	0001 0101		[RESERVED]	42	0100 0010	B	
16	0001 0110		[RESERVED]	43	0100 0011	C	
17	0001 0111		[RESERVED]	44	0100 0100	D	
18	0001 1000		[RESERVED]	45	0100 0101	E	
19	0001 1001		[RESERVED]	46	0100 0110	F	
1A	0001 1010		[RESERVED]	47	0100 0111	G	
1B	0001 1011	ESC	ESCAPE	48	0100 1000	H	
1C	0001 1100		[RESERVED]	49	0100 1001	I	
1D	0001 1101	GS	RECORD TERMINATOR	4A	0100 1010	J	
1E	0001 1110	RS	FIELD TERMINATOR	4B	0100 1011	K	
1F	0001 1111	US	SUBFIELD DELIMITER	4C	0100 1100	L	
20	0010 0000		SPACE (BLANK)	4D	0100 1101	M	
21	0010 0001	!	EXCLAMATION MARK	4E	0100 1110	N	
22	0010 0010	"	QUOTATION MARK	4F	0100 1111	O	
23	0010 0011	#	NUMBER SIGN	50	0101 0000	P	
24	0010 0100	$	DOLLAR SIGN	51	0101 0001	Q	
25	0010 0101	%	PERCENT SIGN	52	0101 0010	R	
26	0010 0110	&	AMPERSAND	53	0101 0011	S	
27	0010 0111	'	APOSTROPHE	54	0101 0100	T	
28	0010 1000	(	OPENING PARENTHESIS	55	0101 0101	U	
29	0010 1001	)	CLOSING PARENTHESIS	56	0101 0110	V	
2A	0010 1010	*	ASTERISK	57	0101 0111	W	
2B	0010 1011	+	PLUS SIGN	58	0101 1000	X	
2C	0010 1100	,	COMMA	59	0101 1001	Y	
2D	0010 1101	-	HYPHEN-MINUS	5A	0101 1010	Z	
2E	0010 1110	.	PERIOD (DECIMAL POINT)	5B	0101 1011	[	OPENING SQUARE BRACKET

Hex	Binary	Graphic	Name/Function	Hex	Binary	Graphic	Name/Function
5C	0101 1100	\	REVERSE SLASH	8E	1000 1110		[RESERVED]
5D	0101 1101	]	CLOSING SQUARE BRACKET	8F	1000 1111		[RESERVED]
5E	0101 1110	^	SPACING CIRCUMFLEX	90	1001 0000		[RESERVED]
5F	0101 1111	_	SPACING UNDERSCORE	91	1001 0001		[RESERVED]
60	0110 0000	`	SPACING GRAVE	92	1001 0010		[RESERVED]
61	0110 0001	a		93	1001 0011		[RESERVED]
62	0110 0010	b		94	1001 0100		[RESERVED]
63	0110 0011	c		95	1001 0101		[RESERVED]
64	0110 0100	d		96	1001 0110		[RESERVED]
65	0110 0101	e		97	1001 0111		[RESERVED]
66	0110 0110	f		98	1001 1000		[RESERVED]
67	0110 0111	g		99	1001 1001		[RESERVED]
68	0110 1000	h		9A	1001 1010		[RESERVED]
69	0110 1001	i		9B	1001 1011		[RESERVED]
6A	0110 1010	j		9C	1001 1100		[RESERVED]
6B	0110 1011	k		9D	1001 1101		[RESERVED]
6C	0110 1100	l		9E	1001 1110		[RESERVED]
6D	0110 1101	m		9F	1001 1111		[RESERVED]
6E	0110 1110	n		A0	1010 0000		[RESERVED]
6F	0110 1111	o		A1	1010 0001	Ł	LOWERCASE POLISH L
70	0111 0000	p		A2	1010 0010	Ø	UPPERCASE SCANDINAVIAN O
71	0111 0001	q		A3	1010 0011	Đ	UPPERCASE D WITH CROSSBAR
72	0111 0010	r		A4	1010 0100	Þ	UPPERCASE ICELANDIC THORN
73	0111 0011	s		A5	1010 0101	Æ	UPPERCASE DIGRAPH AE
74	0111 0100	t		A6	1010 0110	Œ	UPPERCASE DIGRAPH OE
75	0111 0101	u		A7	1010 0111	′	SOFT SIGN (PRIME)
76	0111 0110	v		A8	1010 1000	·	DOT IN MIDDLE OF LINE
77	0111 0111	w		A9	1010 1001	♭	MUSICAL FLAT
78	0111 1000	x		AA	1010 1010	®	SUBSCRIPT PATENT MARK
79	0111 1001	y		AB	1010 1011	±	PLUS OR MINUS
7A	0111 1010	z		AC	1010 1100	Ơ	UPPERCASE O-HOOK
7B	0111 1011	{	OPENING CURLY BRACKET	AD	1010 1101	Ư	UPPERCASE U-HOOK
7C	0111 1100	|	VERTICAL BAR (FILL)	AE	1010 1110	'	ALIF
7D	0111 1101	}	CLOSING CURLY BRACKET	AF	1010 1111		[RESERVED]
7E	0111 1110	~	SPACING TILDE	B0	1011 0000	'	AYN
7F	0111 1111		[RESERVED]	B1	1011 0001	ł	LOWERCASE POLISH L
80	1000 0000		[RESERVED]	B2	1011 0010	ø	LOWERCASE SCANDINAVIAN O
81	1000 0001		[RESERVED]	B3	1011 0011	đ	LOWERCASE D WITH CROSSBAR
82	1000 0010		[RESERVED]	B4	1011 0100	þ	LOWERCASE ICELANDIC THORN
83	1000 0011		[RESERVED]	B5	1011 0101	æ	LOWERCASE DIGRAPH AE
84	1000 0100		[RESERVED]	B6	1011 0110	œ	LOWERCASE DIGRAPH OE
85	1000 0101		[RESERVED]	B7	1011 0111	″	HARD SIGN (DOUBLE PRIME)
86	1000 0110		[RESERVED]	B8	1011 1000	ı	LOWERCASE TURKISH I
87	1000 0111		[RESERVED]	B9	1011 1001	£	BRITISH POUND
88	1000 1000		[RESERVED]	BA	1011 1010	ð	LOWERCASE ETH
89	1000 1001		[RESERVED]	BB	1011 1011		[RESERVED]
8A	1000 1010		[RESERVED]	BC	1011 1100	ơ	LOWERCASE O-HOOK
8B	1000 1011		[RESERVED]	BD	1011 1101	ư	LOWERCASE U-HOOK
8C	1000 1100		[RESERVED]	BE	1011 1110		[RESERVED]
8D	1000 1101		[RESERVED]	BF	1011 1111		[RESERVED]

Hex	Binary	Graphic	Name/Function	Hex	Binary	Graphic	Name/Function
C0	1100 0000	°	DEGREE SIGN	F2	1111 0010	.	DOT BELOW
C1	1100 0001	ℓ	LOWERCASE SCRIPT L	F3	1111 0011	..	DOUBLE DOT BELOW
C2	1100 0010	℗	PHONO COPYRIGHT MARK	F4	1111 0100	°	CIRCLE BELOW
C3	1100 0011	©	COPYRIGHT MARK	F5	1111 0101	=	DOUBLE UNDERSCORE
C4	1100 0100	#	SHARP	F6	1111 0110	_	UNDERSCORE
C5	1100 0101	¿	INVERTED QUESTION MARK	F7	1111 0111	ˌ	LEFT HOOK (COMMA BELOW)
C6	1100 0110	¡	INVERTED EXCLAMATION MARK	F8	1111 1000	¸	RIGHT CEDILLA
C7	1100 0111		[RESERVED]	F9	1111 1001	˘	UPADHMANIYA
C8	1100 1000		[RESERVED]	FA	1111 1010	⌒	DOUBLE TILDE, FIRST HALF
C9	1100 1001		[RESERVED]	FB	1111 1011	⌣	DOUBLE TILDE, SECOND HALF
CA	1100 1010		[RESERVED]	FC	1111 1100		[RESERVED]
CB	1100 1011		[RESERVED]	FD	1111 1101	,	[RESERVED]
CC	1100 1100		[RESERVED]	FE	1111 1110		HIGH COMMA, CENTERED
CD	1100 1101		[RESERVED]	FF	1111 1111		[RESERVED]
CE	1100 1110		[RESERVED]				
CF	1100 1111		[RESERVED]				
D0	1101 0000		[RESERVED]				
D1	1101 0001		[RESERVED]				
D2	1101 0010		[RESERVED]				
D3	1101 0011		[RESERVED]				
D4	1101 0100		[RESERVED]				
D5	1101 0101		[RESERVED]				
D6	1101 0110		[RESERVED]				
D7	1101 0111		[RESERVED]				
D8	1101 1000		[RESERVED]				
D9	1101 1001		[RESERVED]				
DA	1101 1010		[RESERVED]				
DB	1101 1011		[RESERVED]				
DC	1101 1100		[RESERVED]				
DD	1101 1101		[RESERVED]				
DE	1101 1110		[RESERVED]				
DF	1101 1111		[RESERVED]				
E0	1110 0000	ˀ	PSEUDO QUESTION MARK				
E1	1110 0001	`	GRAVE				
E2	1110 0010	´	ACUTE				
E3	1110 0011	^	CIRCUMFLEX				
E4	1110 0100	~	TILDE				
E5	1110 0101	¯	MACRON				
E6	1110 0110	˘	BREVE				
E7	1110 0111	·	SUPERIOR DOT				
E8	1110 1000	¨	UMLAUT (DIAERESIS)				
E9	1110 1001	ˇ	HACEK				
EA	1110 1010	°	CIRCLE ABOVE (ANGSTROM)				
EB	1110 1011	⌒	LIGATURE, FIRST HALF				
EC	1110 1100	⌒	LIGATURE, SECOND HALF				
ED	1110 1101	'	HIGH COMMA, OFF CENTER				
EE	1110 1110	″	DOUBLE ACUTE				
EF	1110 1111	˘	CANDRABINDU				
F0	1111 0000	¸	CEDILLA				
F1	1111 0001	˛	RIGHT HOOK (OGONEK)				

Table 2: Greek Symbols Code Table (8-bit)

Bits 8,7→			00				01				10				11			
Bits 6,5→			00	01	10	11	00	01	10	11	00	01	10	11	00	01	10	11
Hex 0→			0	1	2	3	4	5	6	7	8	9	A	B	C	D	E	F
00	00	0																
	01	1							α									
	10	2							β									
	11	3							γ									
01	00	4																
	01	5																
	10	6																
	11	7																
10	00	8																
	01	9																
	10	A																
	11	B																
11	00	C																
	01	D																
	10	E																
	11	F																

↑   ↑   ↑

4,3 2,1 0   ↑

Bits   Hex   G0 (Greek)

Table 3: Subscript Character Code Table (8-bit)

Bits 8,7→			00				01				10				11			
Bits 6,5→			00	01	10	11	00	01	10	11	00	01	10	11	00	01	10	11
Hex 1→			0	1	2	3	4	5	6	7	8	9	A	B	C	D	E	F
00	00	0				0												
	01	1				1												
	10	2				2												
	11	3				3												
01	00	4				4												
	01	5				5												
	10	6				6												
	11	7				7												
10	00	8			(	8												
	01	9			)	9												
	10	A																
	11	B			+													
11	00	C																
	01	D			-													
	10	E																
	11	F																

↑ ↑ ↑

4,3 2,1 0

Bits Hex G0 (Subscript)

Table 4: Superscript Character Code Table (8-bit)

Bits 8,7→			00				01				10				11			
Bits 6,5→			00	01	10	11	00	01	10	11	00	01	10	11	00	01	10	11
Hex 1→			0	1	2	3	4	5	6	7	8	9	A	B	C	D	E	F
00	00	0				0												
	01	1				1												
	10	2				2												
	11	3				3												
01	00	4				4												
	01	5				5												
	10	6				6												
	11	7				7												
10	00	8			(	8												
	01	9			)	9												
	10	A																
	11	B			+													
11	00	C																
	01	D			-													
	10	E																
	11	F																

↑	↑	↑																
4,3	2,1	0							↑									
Bits	Hex					G0 (Superscript)												

List for Greek Symbols, Subscripts and Superscripts (8-bit)

GREEK SYMBOLS

Hex	Binary	Graphic	Name
61	0110 0001	α	ALPHA
62	0110 0010	β	BETA
63	0110 0011	γ	GAMMA

SUBSCRIPTS

Hex	Binary	Graphic	Name
30	0011 0000	0	SUBSCRIPT 0
31	0011 0001	1	SUBSCRIPT 1
32	0011 0010	2	SUBSCRIPT 2
33	0011 0011	3	SUBSCRIPT 3
34	0011 0100	4	SUBSCRIPT 4
35	0011 0101	5	SUBSCRIPT 5
36	0011 0110	6	SUBSCRIPT 6
37	0011 0111	7	SUBSCRIPT 7
38	0011 1000	8	SUBSCRIPT 8
39	0011 1001	9	SUBSCRIPT 9
28	0010 1000	(	SUBSCRIPT OPENING PARENTHESIS
29	0010 1001	)	SUBSCRIPT CLOSING PARENTHESIS
2B	0010 1011	+	SUBSCRIPT PLUS SIGN
2D	0010 1101	-	SUBSCRIPT HYPHEN-MINUS

SUPERSCRIPTS

Hex	Binary	Graphic	Name
30	0011 0000	0	SUPERSCRIPT 0
31	0011 0001	1	SUPERSCRIPT 1
32	0011 0010	2	SUPERSCRIPT 2
33	0011 0011	3	SUPERSCRIPT 3
34	0011 0100	4	SUPERSCRIPT 4
35	0011 0101	5	SUPERSCRIPT 5
36	0011 0110	6	SUPERSCRIPT 6
37	0011 0111	7	SUPERSCRIPT 7
38	0011 1000	8	SUPERSCRIPT 8
39	0011 1001	9	SUPERSCRIPT 9
28	0010 1000	(	SUPERSCRIPT OPENING PARENTHESIS
29	0010 1001	)	SUPERSCRIPT CLOSING PARENTHESIS
2B	0010 1011	+	SUPERSCRIPT PLUS SIGN
2D	0010 1101	-	SUPERSCRIPT HYPHEN-MINUS

Table 5: Basic Hebrew Character Set (8-bit)

Bits 8,7→			00				01				10				11			
Bits 6,5→			00	01	10	11	00	01	10	11	00	01	10	11	00	01	10	11
Hex 1→			0	1	2	3	4	5	6	7	8	9	A	B	C	D	E	F
00	00	0				0	◌		א	נ								
	01	1			!	1	◌		ב	ס								
	10	2			"	2	◌		ג	ע								
	11	3			#	3	◌		ד	ף								
01	00	4			$	4	◌		ה	פ								
	01	5			%	5	◌		ו	ץ								
	10	6			&	6	◌		ז	צ								
	11	7			’	7	◌		ח	ק								
10	00	8			)	8	◌		ט	ר								
	01	9			(	9	◌		י	ש								
	10	A			*	:	◌		ך	ת								
	11	B			+	;	◌	]	כ	וו								
11	00	C			,	>	◌		ל	וי								
	01	D			-	=	◌	[	ם	יי								
	10	E			.	<	◌		מ									
	11	F			\	?			ן									
↑	↑	↑																
4,3	2,1	0							↑									
Bits	Hex								G0 (Hebrew)									

Note: In the table above the Basic Hebrew character set is shown designated as the G0 set. An agency implementing this character set may choose to designate it as either a G0 or G1 set, in which case the value of *bit 8* must be adjusted. Bits 1 through 7 may not vary.

Code List for the Basic Hebrew Character Set (8-bit)

Hex	Binary	Graphic	Name/Function	Hex	Binary	Graphic	Name/Function
21	0010 0001	!	EXCLAMATION MARK	50	0101 0000		[RESERVED]
22	0010 0010	"	QUOTATION MARK	51	0101 0001		[RESERVED]
23	0010 0011	#	NUMBER SIGN	52	0101 0010		[RESERVED]
24	0010 0100	$	DOLLAR SIGN	53	0101 0011		[RESERVED]
25	0010 0101	%	PERCENT SIGN	54	0101 0100		[RESERVED]
26	0010 0110	&	AMPERSAND	55	0101 0101		[RESERVED]
27	0010 0111	'	APOSTROPHE	56	0101 0110		[RESERVED]
28	0010 1000	)	OPENING PARENTHESIS	57	0101 0111		[RESERVED]
29	0010 1001	(	CLOSING PARENTHESIS	58	0101 1000		[RESERVED]
2A	0010 1010	*	ASTERISK	59	0101 1001		[RESERVED]
2B	0010 1011	+	PLUS SIGN	5A	0101 1010		[RESERVED]
2C	0010 1100	,	COMMA	5B	0101 1011	]	OPENING BRACKET
2D	0010 1101	-	HYPHEN-MINUS	5C	0101 1100		[RESERVED]
2E	0010 1110	.	PERIOD (DECIMAL POINT)	5D	0101 1101	[	CLOSING BRACKET
2F	0010 1111	\	SLASH	5E	0101 1110		[RESERVED]
30	0011 0000	0		5F	0101 1111		[RESERVED]
31	0011 0001	1		60	0110 0000	א	ALEF
32	0011 0010	2		61	0110 0001	ב	BET (UNMARKED)
33	0011 0011	3		62	0110 0010	ג	GIMEL
34	0011 0100	4		63	0110 0011	ד	DALET
35	0011 0101	5		64	0110 0100	ה	HE
36	0011 0110	6		65	0110 0101	ו	VAV
37	0011 0111	7		66	0110 0110	ז	ZAYIN
38	0011 1000	8		67	0110 0111	ח	HET
39	0011 1001	9		68	0110 1000	ט	TET
3A	0011 1010	:	COLON	69	0110 1001	י	YOD
3B	0011 1011	;	SEMICOLON	6A	0110 1010	ך	FINAL KAF (SOFIT)
3C	0011 1100	>	OPENING ANGLE BRACKET	6B	0110 1011	כ	KAF
3D	0011 1101	=	EQUAL SIGN	6C	0110 1100	ל	LAMED
3E	0011 1110	<	CLOSING ANGLE BRACKET	6D	0110 1101	ם	FINAL MEM (SOFIT)
3F	0011 1111	?	QUESTION MARK	6E	0110 1110	מ	MEM
40	0100 0000	◌	PATAH	6F	0110 1111	ן	FINAL NUN (SOFIT)
41	0100 0001	◌	KAMATS	70	0111 0000	נ	NUN
42	0100 0010	◌	SEGOL	71	0111 0001	ס	SAMEKH
43	0100 0011	◌	TSEREH	72	0111 0010	ע	'AYIN
44	0100 0100	◌	HIRIK	73	0111 0011	ף	FINAL PE (SOFIT)
45	0100 0101	◌	HOLAM	74	0111 0100	פ	PE
46	0100 0110	◌	KUBUTS	75	0111 0101	ץ	FINAL TSADI (SOFIT)
47	0100 0111	◌	SHEVA	76	0111 0110	צ	TSADI
48	0100 1000	◌	HATAF PATAH	77	0111 0111	ק	KOF
49	0100 1001	◌	HATAF KAMATS	78	0111 1000	ר	RESH
4A	0100 1010	◌	HATAF SEGOL	79	0111 1001	ש	SHIN (UNMARKED)
4B	0100 1011	◌	DAGESH	7A	0111 1010	ת	TAV (UNMARKED)
4C	0100 1100	◌	RAFEH	7B	0111 1011	וו	TSVEY VOVN
4D	0100 1101	◌	RIGHT SHIN DOT	7C	0111 1100	וי	VOV YUD
4E	0100 1110	◌	VARIKA	7D	0111 1101	יי	TSVEY YUDN
4F	0100 1111		[RESERVED]	7E	0111 1110		[RESERVED]

Table 6: Basic Cyrillic and Extended Cyrillic Character Sets (8-bit)

Bits 8,7→			00				01				10				11			
Bits 6,5→			00	01	10	11	00	01	10	11	00	01	10	11	00	01	10	11
Hex 1→			0	1	2	3	4	5	6	7	8	9	A	B	C	D	E	F
00	00	0				0	ю	п	Ю	П					г	ђ	Ґ	Ђ
	01	1			!	1	а	я	А	Я					ђ	ө	Ђ	Ө
	10	2			"	2	б	р	Б	Р					ѓ	v	Ѓ	V
	11	3			#	3	ц	с	Ц	С					є	ѫ	Є	Ѫ
01	00	4			$	4	д	т	Д	Т					ё		Ё	
	01	5			%	5	е	у	Е	У					ѕ		Ѕ	
	10	6			&	6	ф	ж	Ф	Ж					і		І	
	11	7			'	7	г	в	Г	В					ї		Ї	
10	00	8			(	8	х	ь	Х	Ь					ј		Ј	
	01	9			)	9	и	ы	И	Ы					љ		Љ	
	10	A			*	:	й	з	Й	З					њ		Њ	
	11	B			+	;	к	ш	К	Ш					ћ	[	Ћ	
11	00	C			,	<	л	э	Л	Э					ќ		Ќ	
	01	D			-	=	м	щ	М	Щ					ў	]	Ў	
	10	E			.	>	н	ч	Н	Ч					џ		Џ	
	11	F			/	?	о	ъ	О								Ъ	
↑ ↑ ↑																		
4,3 2,1 0							↑								↑			
Bits Hex						G0 (Basic Cyrillic)						G1 (Extended Cyrillic)						

Note: In the table above the Basic Cyrillic character set is shown designated as the G0 set and the Extended Cyrillic character set as the G1 set. An agency implementing either character set may choose to designate the Basic Cyrillic character set or the Extended Cyrillic character set as either a G0 or G1 set, in which case the value of *bit 8* must be adjusted. Bits 1 through 7 may not vary.

Code List for the Basic and Extended Cyrillic Character Sets (8-bit)

Hex	Binary	Graphic	Name/Function	Hex	Binary	Graphic	Name/Function
21	0010 0001	!	EXCLAMATION MARK	4E	0100 1110	н	LOWERCASE EN
22	0010 0010	"	QUOTATION MARK	4F	0100 1111	о	LOWERCASE O
23	0010 0011	#	NUMBER SIGN	50	0101 0000	п	LOWERCASE PE
24	0010 0100	$	DOLLAR SIGN	51	0101 0001	я	LOWERCASE IA
25	0010 0101	%	PERCENT SIGN	52	0101 0010	р	LOWERCASE ER
26	0010 0110	&	AMPERSAND	53	0101 0011	с	LOWERCASE ES
27	0010 0111	'	APOSTROPHE	54	0101 0100	т	LOWERCASE TE
28	0010 1000	(	OPENING PARENTHESIS	55	0101 0101	у	LOWERCASE U
29	0010 1001	)	CLOSING PARENTHESIS	56	0101 0110	ж	LOWERCASE ZHE
2A	0010 1010	*	ASTERISK	57	0101 0111	в	LOWERCASE VE
2B	0010 1011	+	PLUS SIGN	58	0101 1000	ь	LOWERCASE SOFT SIGN
2C	0010 1100	,	COMMA				(LOWERCASE BULGARIAN U)
2D	0010 1101	-	HYPHEN-MINUS	59	0101 1001	ы	LOWERCASE YERI
2E	0010 1110	.	PERIOD (DECIMAL POINT)	5A	0101 1010	з	LOWERCASE ZE
2F	0010 1111	/	SLASH	5B	0101 1011	ш	LOWERCASE SHA
30	0011 0000	0		5C	0101 1100	э	LOWERCASE REVERSED E
31	0011 0001	1		5D	0101 1101	щ	LOWERCASE SHCHA
32	0011 0010	2		5E	0101 1110	ч	LOWERCASE CHE
33	0011 0011	3		5F	0101 1111	ъ	LOWERCASE HARD SIGN
34	0011 0100	4		60	0110 0000	Ю	UPPERCASE IU
35	0011 0101	5		61	0110 0001	А	UPPERCASE A
36	0011 0110	6		62	0110 0010	Б	UPPERCASE BE
37	0011 0111	7		63	0110 0011	Ц	UPPERCASE TSE
38	0011 1000	8		64	0110 0100	Д	UPPERCASE DE
39	0011 1001	9		65	0110 0101	Е	UPPERCASE IE
3A	0011 1010	:	COLON	66	0110 0110	Ф	UPPERCASE EF
3B	0011 1011	;	SEMICOLON	67	0110 0111	Г	UPPERCASE GE
3C	0011 1100	<	LESS-THAN SIGN	68	0110 1000	Х	UPPERCASE KHA
			(OPENING ANGLE BRACKET)	69	0110 1001	И	UPPERCASE II
3D	0011 1101	=	EQUAL SIGN	6A	0110 1010	Й	UPPERCASE SHORT II
3E	0011 1110	>	GREATER-THAN SIGN	6B	0110 1011	К	UPPERCASE KA
			(CLOSING ANGLE BRACKET)	6C	0110 1100	Л	UPPERCASE EL
3F	0011 1111	?	QUESTION MARK	6D	0110 1101	М	UPPERCASE EM
40	0100 0000	ю	LOWERCASE IU	6E	0110 1110	Н	UPPERCASE EN
41	0100 0001	а	LOWERCASE A	6F	0110 1111	О	UPPERCASE O
42	0100 0010	б	LOWERCASE BE	70	0111 0000	П	UPPERCASE PE
43	0100 0011	ц	LOWERCASE TSE	71	0111 0001	Я	UPPERCASE IA
44	0100 0100	д	LOWERCASE DE	72	0111 0010	Р	UPPERCASE ER
45	0100 0101	е	LOWERCASE IE	73	0111 0011	С	UPPERCASE ES
46	0100 0110	ф	LOWERCASE EF	74	0111 0100	Т	UPPERCASE TE
47	0100 0111	г	LOWERCASE GE	75	0111 0101	У	UPPERCASE U
48	0100 1000	х	LOWERCASE KHA	76	0111 0110	Ж	UPPERCASE ZHE
49	0100 1001	и	LOWERCASE II	77	0111 0111	В	UPPERCASE VE
4A	0100 1010	й	LOWERCASE SHORT II	78	0111 1000	Ь	UPPERCASE SOFT SIGN
4B	0100 1011	к	LOWERCASE KA	79	0111 1001	Ы	UPPERCASE YERI
4C	0100 1100	л	LOWERCASE EL	7A	0111 1010	З	UPPERCASE ZE
4D	0100 1101	м	LOWERCASE EM	7B	0111 1011	Ш	UPPERCASE SHA

Hex	Binary	Graphic	Name/Function	Hex	Binary	Graphic	Name/Function
7C	0111 1100	Э	UPPERCASE REVERSED E	D0	1101 0000	ѣ	LOWERCASE YAT
7D	0111 1101	Щ	UPPERCASE SHCHA	D1	1101 0001	ѳ	LOWERCASE FITA
7E	0111 1110	Ч	UPPERCASE CHA	D2	1101 0010	ѵ	LOWERCASE IZHITSA
A1	1010 0001		[RESERVED]	D3	1101 0011	ѫ	LOWERCASE BIG YUS
A2	1010 0010		[RESERVED]	D4	1101 0100		[RESERVED]
A3	1010 0011		[RESERVED]	D5	1101 0101		[RESERVED]
A4	1010 0100		[RESERVED]	D6	1101 0110		[RESERVED]
A5	1010 0101		[RESERVED]	D7	1101 0111		[RESERVED]
A6	1010 0110		[RESERVED]	D8	1101 1000		[RESERVED]
A7	1010 0111		[RESERVED]	D9	1101 1001		[RESERVED]
A8	1010 1000		[RESERVED]	DA	1101 1010		[RESERVED]
A9	1010 1001		[RESERVED]	DB	1101 1011	[	OPENING BRACKET
AA	1010 1010		[RESERVED]	DC	1101 1100		[RESERVED]
AB	1010 1011		[RESERVED]	DD	1101 1101	]	CLOSING BRACKET
AC	1010 1100		[RESERVED]	DE	1101 1110		[RESERVED]
AD	1010 1101		[RESERVED]	DF	1101 1111		[RESERVED]
AE	1010 1110		[RESERVED]	E0	1110 0000	Ґ	UPPERCASE G WITH UPTURN
AF	1010 1111		[RESERVED]	E1	1110 0001	Ђ	UPPERCASE DJE
B0	1011 0000		[RESERVED]	E2	1110 0010	Ѓ	UPPERCASE GJE
B1	1011 0001		[RESERVED]	E3	1110 0011	Є	UPPERCASE E
B2	1011 0010		[RESERVED]	E4	1110 0100	Ё	UPPERCASE IO
B3	1011 0011		[RESERVED]	E5	1110 0101	Ѕ	UPPERCASE DZE
B4	1011 0100		[RESERVED]	E6	1110 0110	І	UPPERCASE I
B5	1011 0101		[RESERVED]	E7	1110 0111	Ї	UPPERCASE YI
B6	1011 0110		[RESERVED]	E8	1110 1000	Ј	UPPERCASE JE
B7	1011 0111		[RESERVED]	E9	1110 1001	Љ	UPPERCASE LJE
B8	1011 1000		[RESERVED]	EA	1110 1010	Њ	UPPERCASE NJE
B9	1011 1001		[RESERVED]	EB	1110 1011	Ћ	UPPERCASE TSHE
BA	1011 1010		[RESERVED]	EC	1110 1100	Ќ	UPPERCASE KJE
BB	1011 1011		[RESERVED]	ED	1110 1101	Ў	UPPERCASE SHORT U
BC	1011 1100		[RESERVED]	EE	1110 1110	Џ	UPPERCASE DZHE
BD	1011 1101		[RESERVED]	EF	1110 1111	Ъ	UPPERCASE HARD SIGN
BE	1011 1110		[RESERVED]				(UPPERCASE BULGARIAN U)
BF	1011 1111		[RESERVED]	F0	1111 0000	Ѣ	UPPERCASE YAT
C0	1100 0000	ґ	LOWERCASE GE WITH UPTURN	F1	1111 0001	Ѳ	UPPERCASE FITA
C1	1100 0001	ђ	LOWERCASE DJE	F2	1111 0010	Ѵ	UPPERCASE IZHITSA
C2	1100 0010	ѓ	LOWERCASE GJE	F3	1111 0011	Ѫ	UPPERCASE BIG YUS
C3	1100 0011	є	LOWERCASE E	F4	1111 0100		[RESERVED]
C4	1100 0100	ё	LOWERCASE IO	F5	1111 0101		[RESERVED]
C5	1100 0101	ѕ	LOWERCASE DZE	F6	1111 0110		[RESERVED]
C6	1100 0110	і	LOWERCASE I	F7	1111 0111		[RESERVED]
C7	1100 0111	ї	LOWERCASE YI	F8	1111 1000		[RESERVED]
C8	1100 1000	ј	LOWERCASE JE	F9	1111 1001		[RESERVED]
C9	1100 1001	љ	LOWERCASE LJE	FA	1111 1010		[RESERVED]
CA	1100 1010	њ	LOWERCASE NJE	FB	1111 1011		[RESERVED]
CB	1100 1011	ћ	LOWERCASE TSHE	FC	1111 1100		[RESERVED]
CC	1100 1100	ќ	LOWERCASE KJE	FD	1111 1101		[RESERVED]
CD	1100 1101	ў	LOWERCASE SHORT U	FE	1111 1110		[RESERVED]
CE	1100 1110	џ	LOWERCASE DZHE				
CF	1100 1111		[RESERVED]				

Table 7: Basic Arabic and Extended Arabic Character Sets (8-bit)

Bits 8,7→			00				01				10				11			
Bits 6,5→			00	01	10	11	00	01	10	11	00	01	10	11	00	01	10	11
Hex 1→			0	1	2	3	4	5	6	7	8	9	A	B	C	D	E	F
00	00	0				•		ذ	—	ـَ				خ	ر	ك	ﯖ	و
	01	1			!	١	ء	ر	ف	ـّ			آ	ج	ر	ب	گ	ؤ
	10	2			"	٢	آ	ز	ق	ٲ			أ	چ	بر	ف	گ	ۇ
	11	3			#	٣	ا	س	ك				إ	ج	ز	ف	ﮒ	ۆ
01	00	4			$	٤	ؤ	ش	ل	ا			ټ	ڬ	ژ	پ	ڶ	ى
	01	5			%	٥	إ	ص	م				ث	ڭ	ز	ة	ڵ	ﯧ
	10	6			&	٦	ئ	ض	ن				ب	د	بس	ف	ﺋ	ﭽ
	11	7			'	٧	ا	ط	ه				تـ	ڈ	پس	ق	ﻝ	ح
10	00	8			)	٨	ب	ظ	و				ت	ذ	ش	ک	ب	ع
	01	9			(	٩	ة	ع	ى				ت	ڊ	ش	ک	ﺖ	ﺓ
	10	A			*	:	ت	غ	ي	≈			ٿ	ذ	ص	گ	ن	ﮐ
	11	B			+	؛	ث	]					ٻ	ذ	ض	ك	ث	
11	00	C			،	>	ج		ﻯ				خ	ذ	ج	ك	ن	
	01	D			-	=	ح	[					خ	ڑ	ظ	پ	ه	▫
	10	E			.	<	خ		ٓ				ج	ڗ	غ	گ	ة	▫
	11	F			\	؟	د		ٔ				ج	ﺮ	غ	گ	و	

↑	↑	↑													
4,3	2,1	0				↑							↑		
Bits		**Hex**				G0 (Basic Arabic)							G1 (Extended Arabic)		

Note: In the table above the Basic Arabic character set is shown designated as the G0 set and the Extended Arabic character set as the G1 set. An agency implementing either character set may choose to designate the Basic Arabic character set or the Extended Arabic character set as either a G0 or G1 set, in which case the value of *bit 8* must be adjusted. Bits 1 through 7 may not vary.

Code List for the Basic Arabic and Extended Arabic Character Sets (8-bit)

Hex	Binary	Graphic	Name/Function	Hex	Binary	Graphic	Name/Function
21	0010 0001	!	EXCLAMATION MARK	48	0100 1000	ب	BEH
22	0010 0010	"	QUOTATION MARK	49	0100 1001	ة	TEH MARBUTA
23	0010 0011	#	NUMBER SIGN	4A	0100 1010	ت	TEH
24	0010 0100	$	DOLLAR SIGN	4B	0100 1011	ث	THEH
25	0010 0101	%	PERCENT SIGN	4C	0100 1100	ج	JEEM
26	0010 0110	&	AMPERSAND	4D	0100 1101	ح	HAH
27	0010 0111	,	APOSTROPHE	4E	0100 1110	خ	KHAH
28	0010 1000	)	OPENING PARENTHESIS	4F	0100 1111	د	DAL
29	0010 1001	(	CLOSING PARENTHESIS	50	0101 0000	ذ	THAL
2A	0010 1010	*	ASTERISK	51	0101 0001	ر	REH
2B	0010 1011	+	PLUS SIGN	52	0101 0010	ز	ZAIN
2C	0010 1100	،	ARABIC COMMA	53	0101 0011	س	SEEN
2D	0010 1101	−	HYPHEN-MINUS	54	0101 0100	ش	SHEEN
2E	0010 1110	.	PERIOD (DECIMAL POINT)	55	0101 0101	ص	SAD
2F	0010 1111	\	SLASH	56	0101 0110	ض	DAD
30	0011 0000	•	ARABIC-INDIC DIGIT ZERO	57	0101 0111	ط	TAH
31	0011 0001	١	ARABIC-INDIC DIGIT ONE	58	0101 1000	ظ	ZAH
32	0011 0010	٢	ARABIC-INDIC DIGIT TWO	59	0101 1001	ع	AIN
33	0011 0011	٣	ARABIC-INDIC DIGIT THREE	5A	0101 1010	غ	GHAIN
34	0011 0100	٤	ARABIC-INDIC DIGIT FOUR	5B	0101 1011	]	OPENING BRACKET
35	0011 0101	٥	ARABIC-INDIC DIGIT FIVE	5C	0101 1100		[RESERVED]
36	0011 0110	٦	ARABIC-INDIC DIGIT SIX	5D	0101 1101	]	CLOSING BRACKET
37	0011 0111	٧	ARABIC-INDIC DIGIT SEVEN	5E	0101 1110		[RESERVED]
38	0011 1000	٨	ARABIC-INDIC DIGIT EIGHT	5F	0101 1111		[RESERVED]
39	0011 1001	٩	ARABIC-INDIC DIGIT NINE	60	0110 0000	ـ	TATWEEL
3A	0011 1010	:	COLON	61	0110 0001	ف	FEH
3B	0011 1011	؛	ARABIC SEMICOLON	62	0110 0010	ق	QAF
3C	0011 1100	>	OPENING ANGLE BRACKET	63	0110 0011	ك	KAF
3D	0011 1101	=	EQUAL SIGN	64	0110 0100	ل	LAM
3E	0011 1110	<	CLOSING ANGLE BRACKET	65	0110 0101	م	MEEM
3F	0011 1111	؟	ARABIC QUESTION MARK	66	0110 0110	ن	NOON
40	0100 0000		[RESERVED]	67	0110 0111	ه	HEH
41	0100 0001	ء	HAMZAH	68	0110 1000	و	WAW
42	0100 0010	آ	ALEF WITH MADDA ABOVE	69	0110 1001	ى	ALEF MAQSURA
43	0100 0011	أ	ALEF WITH HAMZA ABOVE	6A	0110 1010	ي	YEH
44	0100 0100	ؤ	WAW WITH HAMZA ABOVE	6B	0110 1011	ً	FATHATAN
45	0100 0101	إ	ALEF WITH HAMZA BELOW	6C	0110 1100	ٌ	DAMMATAN
46	0100 0110	ئ	YEH WITH HAMZA ABOVE	6D	0110 1101	ٍ	KASRATAN
47	0100 0111	ا	ALEF	6E	0110 1110	َ	FATHA

Hex	Binary	Graphic	Name/Function	Hex	Binary	Graphic	Name/Function
6F	0110 1111	ٌ	DAMMA	B7	1011 0111	ڟ	DAL WITH DOT BELOW AND
70	0111 0000	ِ	KASRA				SMALL TAH
71	0111 0001	ّ	SHADDA	B8	1011 1000	ذ	DAHAL
72	0111 0010	ْ	SUKUN	B9	1011 1001	ڊ	DDAHAL
73	0111 0011	ٱ	ALEF WASLA	BA	1011 1010	ڎ	DUL
74	0111 0100	ٰ	SUPERSCRIPT ALEF	BB	1011 1011	ڋ	DAL WITH THREE DOTS ABOVE
75	0111 0101		[RESERVED]				DOWNWARDS
76	0111 0110		[RESERVED]	BC	1011 1100	ڌ	DAL WITH FOUR DOTS ABOVE
77	0111 0111		[RESERVED]	BD	1011 1101	ڑ	RREH
78	0111 1000		[RESERVED]	BE	1011 1110	ڔ	REH WITH SMALL V
79	0111 1001		[RESERVED]	BF	1011 1111	ڕ	REH WITH RING
7A	0111 1010		[RESERVED]	C0	1100 0000	ڒ	REH WITH DOT BELOW
7B	0111 1011		[RESERVED]	C1	1100 0001	ڕ	REH WITH SMALL V BELOW
7C	0111 1100		[RESERVED]	C2	1100 0010	ڗ	REH WITH DOT ABOVE AND
7D	0111 1101		[RESERVED]				BELOW
7E	0111 1110		[RESERVED]	C3	1100 0011	ڒ	REH WITH TWO DOTS ABOVE
A1	1010 0001	آ	DOUBLE ALEF WITH HAMZA	C4	1100 0100	ژ	JEH
			ABOVE	C5	1100 0101	ڙ	REH WITH FOUR DOTS ABOVE
A2	1010 0010	أ	ALEF WITH WAVY HAMZA	C6	1100 0110	ښ	SEEN WITH DOT BELOW AND
			ABOVE				DOT ABOVE
A3	1010 0011	إ	ALEF WITH WAVY HAMZA	C7	1100 0111	ڛ	SEEN WITH THREE DOTS BELOW
			BELOW	C8	1100 1000	ڜ	SHEEN WITH THREE DOTS BELOW
A4	1010 0100	ٹ	TTEH	C9	1100 1001	ڝ	SHEEN WITH DOT BELOW
A5	1010 0101	ٿ	TTEHEH	CA	1100 1010	ڞ	SAD WITH TWO DOTS BELOW
A6	1010 0110	ٻ	BBEH	CB	1100 1011	ض	SAD WITH THREE DOTS ABOVE
A7	1010 0111	ٿ	TEH WITH RING	CC	1100 1100	ڞ	DAD WITH DOT BELOW
A8	1010 1000	ٺ	TEH WITH THREE DOTS ABOVE	CD	1100 1101	ظ	TAH WITH THREE DOTS ABOVE
A9	1010 1001	پ	PEH	CE	1100 1110	ڠ	AIN WITH THREE DOTS ABOVE
AA	1010 1010	ٹ	TEHEH	CF	1100 1111	غ	GHAIN WITH DOT BELOW
AB	1010 1011	ڀ	BEHEH	D0	1101 0000	ڡ	DOTLESS FEH
AC	1010 1100	ڇ	HAH WITH HAMZA ABOVE	D1	1101 0001	ڢ	FEH WITH DOT MOVED BELOW
AD	1010 1101	ڿ	HAH WITH TWO DOTS VERTICAL	D2	1101 0010	ڣ	FEH WITH DOT BELOW
			ABOVE	D3	1101 0011	ڤ	VEH
AE	1010 1110	ڃ	NYEH	D4	1101 0100	ڦ	FEH WITH THREE DOTS BELOW
AF	1010 1111	ج	DYEH	D5	1101 0101	ڥ	PEHEH
B0	1011 0000	ڂ	HAH WITH THREE DOTS ABOVE	D6	1101 0110	ڧ	QAF WITH DOT ABOVE
B1	1011 0001	چ	TCHEH	D7	1101 0111	ڨ	QAF WITH THREE DOTS ABOVE
B2	1011 0010	ڇ	TCHEH WITH DOT ABOVE	D8	1101 1000	ک	KEHEH
B3	1011 0011	ڃ	TCHEHEH	D9	1101 1001	ڪ	SWASH KAF
B4	1011 0100	ڈ	DDAL	DA	1101 1010	گ	KAF WITH RING
B5	1011 0101	ڊ	DAL WITH RING	DB	1101 1011	ڬ	KAF WITH DOT ABOVE
B6	1011 0110	ڊ	DAL WITH DOT BELOW	DC	1101 1100	ڭ	NG

Hex Binary Graphic Name/Function

Hex	Binary	Graphic	Name/Function
DD	1101 1101	ڭ	KAF WITH THREE DOTS BELOW
DE	1101 1110	گ	GAF
DF	1101 1111	گ	GAF WITH RING
E0	1110 0000	ڭ	NGOEH
E1	1110 0001	ڮ	GAF WITH TWO DOTS BELOW
E2	1110 0010	ڲ	GUEH
E3	1110 0011	ڰ	GAF WITH THREE DOTS ABOVE
E4	1110 0100	ڵ	LAM WITH SMALL V
E5	1110 0101	ڶ	LAM WITH DOT ABOVE
E6	1110 0110	ڷ	LAM WITH THREE DOTS ABOVE
E7	1110 0111	ڸ	LAM WITH THREE DOTS BELOW
E8	1110 1000	ں	NOON GHUNNA
E9	1110 1001	ٹ	RNOON
EA	1110 1010	ڹ	NOON WITH RING
EB	1110 1011	ث	NOON WITH THREE DOTS ABOVE
EC	1110 1100	ڻ	NOON WITH DOT BELOW
ED	1110 1101	ھ	HEH DOACHASHMEE
EE	1110 1110	ة	HEH WITH HAMZA ABOVE
EF	1110 1111	ۅ	WAW WITH RING
F0	1111 0000	ۄ	KYRGHYZ OE
F1	1111 0001	ۆ	OE
F2	1111 0010	ۊ	WAW WITH TWO DOTS
F3	1111 0011	ۏ	VE
F4	1111 0100	ى	YEH WITH TAIL
F5	1111 0101	ێ	YEH WITH SMALL V
F6	1111 0110	ې	E
F7	1111 0111	ے	YEH BARREE
F8	1111 1000	ۓ	YEH BARREE WITH HAMZA ABOVE
F9	1111 1001		[RESERVED]
FA	1111 1010		[RESERVED]
FB	1111 1011		[RESERVED]
FC	1111 1100		[RESERVED]
FD	1111 1101	ٗ	SHORT E
FE	1111 1110	ٗ	SHORT U

INTRODUCTION

The use of an exchange medium (e.g., tape, diskette) is an integral part of sharing USMARC records. This section includes media format and labelling specifications for magnetic tape, microcomputer diskettes, and electronic file transfer which are now being used to exchange USMARC data. The specifications vary slightly for each medium to allow better utilization of the technology involved. Adherence to media format and labelling specifications is essential for successful exchange of USMARC records.

DEFINITIONS

Italicized terms within definitions are terms for which definitions are also provided.

bibliographic file. A *file* on the exchange medium (e.g., *tape*, *diskette*) that contains MARC records. When generally used, the term can refer to MARC records containing authority, bibliographic, classification, community information, and holdings data.

blank. ASCII character 20_{16} (represented graphically in USMARC documentation as ƀ). Also referred to as the space character.

block. A collection of contiguously recorded characters written or read as a unit. Blocks are separated by an *interblock gap*. A block may contain one or more complete *records*, or it may contain segments of one or more *segmented records*. A block does not contain multiple segments of the same record.

blocked record. A *record* contained in a *file* in which each *block* may contain more than one record or *record segment*.

data element. A defined unit of information.

diskette. A physical exchange medium usually composed of a thin disk with a magnetic surface on both sides, enclosed in protective case. A variety of diskette sizes exist, 5.25 inches or 3.5 inches in diameter being the most common. Hardware to read from and write to such diskettes usually support various densities of encoded data.

field. A defined character string that may contain one or more *data elements*.

file. A set of related *records* treated as a unit. A file may form part of a physical or logical *volume*.

file section. That part of a *file* that is recorded on any one *volume*. The sections of a file do not have sections of other files interspersed.

file transfer protocol (FTP). A standard technique and syntax for communicating machine-readable data electronically in separate files without losing data or file integrity.

interblock gap. A magnetically-erased section of tape separating *blocks* of information.

label. A *record* at the beginning of a *volume*, and at the beginning and end of a *file section*, that identifies and characterizes that volume and file section. A label is not considered to be part of a file section. A label is identified by a three letter Label Identifier followed by a single character, the Label Number. Each label is recorded in a separate *block*.

label file. *File* on an exchange medium that identifies and characterizes the content of the *file(s)* and/or *volume(s)*.

label group. One or more contiguous *label sets*.

label set. One or more contiguous *labels* with the same three initial characters (Label Identifier).

originating system. An information processing system that writes *files* of MARC records for the purpose of data interchange with a *receiving system*.

receiving system. An information processing system that is intended to read *files* of MARC records that have been processed by an *originating system* for the purpose of data interchange.

record. Related pieces of data treated as a unit.

record segment. That part of a *segmented record* that is contained in any one *block*. The segments of a record do not have segments of other records interspersed.

segment control word (SCW). A fixed-length string used to indicate the type and content of a segment in a *file* of *segmented records*.

segmented record. A *record* contained in a *file* in which each record consists of a sequence of one or more *record segments*. Records are contained in one or more consecutive *blocks*, such that only one segment of each record can appear in any one block.

tape. A physical exchange medium usually composed of a thin acetate film in a variety of widths (2-inch (5.08cm), 1-inch (2.54cm), and ½-inch (1.27cm) tape are the most common). The acetate film can be housed on reels or in cartridges.

tape mark. A special control block recorded on magnetic tape to serve as a separator between *file sections* and *label groups* and also between certain label groups.

transaction. A single operation in which a *volume* or set of volumes of MARC *file(s)* is transferred from an *originating system* to a *receiving system*.

volume. A physical or logical unit which includes part of a *file*, a complete file, or more than one file. For separate (dismountable) media (e.g., a reel of magnetic tape), a volume is usually a single physical unit. A volume contains *label file(s)* and one or more *bibliographic file(s)*. It may contain sections of files but does not contain multiple sections of the same file.

Current Tape Specifications

The specifications for the formatting and labeling of magnetic tape currently used in the distribution of USMARC authority, bibliographic, classification, community information, and holdings records are described below. These specifications have been used since the end of 1977 and are based on *Magnetic Tape Labels and File Structure for Information Interchange* (ANSI X3.27, 1978 edition, or later), *Recorded Magnetic Tape for Information Interchange (1600 CPI, PE)* (ANSI X3.39), and *Recorded Magnetic Tape for Information Interchange (6250 CPI, Group-Coded Recording)* (ANSI X3.54). They supersede the pre-1977 tape specifications which are described later.

Tape Format

USMARC magnetic tape reels and tape cartridges are nine channel tapes (odd parity) written at 1600, 6250, or 38,000 characters per inch. USMARC tapes contain internal labels written in ASCII. Each label is an 80-byte record, the byte positions of which are numbered, starting with the leftmost byte position, 0 to 79. Each label occupies a separate 2048-character file segment (1968 characters of which are padding blanks), without any **Segment Control Word**. (Refer to the section on record segmentation for more information on the use of the Segment Control Word in segments containing USMARC records.) Each file of records is terminated by a tape mark.

Tape File Organization

Files may be organized on tape in volumes in one of four ways: 1) single volume, single file; 2) single volume, multiple files; 3) multiple volumes, single file; and 4) multiple volumes, multiple files. Examples of the sequence of labels, tape marks and files for each configuration is given below.

Single volume, Single file

Volume Header Label (VOL1)
File Header Label (HDR1)
File Header Label (HDR2)
  Tape Mark
File of data records
  Tape Mark
End of File Label (EOF1)
End of File Label (EOF2)
  Tape Mark
  Tape Mark

Single volume, Multiple files

Volume Header Label (VOL1)
File Header Label (HDR1)
File Header Label (HDR2)
  Tape Mark
File A of data records
  Tape Mark
End of File Label (EOF1)
End of File Label (EOF2)
  Tape Mark
File Header Label (HDR1)
File Header Label (HDR2)
  Tape Mark
File B of data records
  Tape Mark
End of File Label (EOF1)
End of File Label (EOF2)
  Tape Mark
  Tape Mark

Multiple volumes, Single file

Volume A	*Volume B*
Volume Header Label (VOL1)	Volume Header Label (VOL1)
File Header Label (HDR1)	File Header Label (HDR1)
File Header Label (HDR2)	File Header Label (HDR2)
Tape Mark	Tape Mark
File of data record-Part 1	File of data records-Part 2
Tape Mark	Tape Mark
End of Volume Label (EOV1)	End of File Label (EOF1)
End of Volume Label (EOV2)	End of File Label (EOF2)
Tape Mark	Tape Mark
Tape Mark	Tape Mark

Multiple volumes, Multiple files

Volume A	*Volume B*	*Volume C*
Volume Header Label (VOL1)	Volume Header Label (VOL1)	Volume Header Label (VOL1)
File Header Label (HDR1)	File Header Label (HDR1)	File Header Label (HDR1)
File Header Label (HDR2)	File Header Label (HDR2)	File Header Label (HDR2)
Tape Mark	Tape Mark	Tape Mark
File A of data records	File B of data records-Pt.2	File B of data records-Pt.3
Tape Mark	Tape Mark	Tape Mark
End of File Label (EOF1)	End of Volume Label (EOV1)	End of File Label (EOF1)
End of File Label (EOF2)	End of Volume Label (EOV2)	End of File Label (EOF2)
Tape Mark	Tape Mark	Tape Mark
File Header Label (HDR1)	Tape Mark	File Header Label (HDR1)
File Header Label (HDR2)		File Header Label (HDR2)
Tape Mark		Tape Mark
File B of data records-Pt.1		File C of data records
Tape Mark		Tape Mark
End of Volume Label (EOV1)		End of File Label (EOF1)
End of Volume Label (EOV2)		End of File Label (EOF2)
Tape Mark		Tape Mark
Tape Mark		Tape Mark

Tape Labels

USMARC tapes contain internal labels that identify and characterize the volume and file section. They occur at the beginning of a volume and at the beginning and end of each file section. Each label is recorded in a separate block. Tapes should be identified on an external eye-readable label by volume and number.

The internal labels appearing on USMARC tapes are described below. The labels may contain ASCII numeric characters 0-9, ASCII uppercase alphabetic characters A-Z, and characters from the following group of ASCII graphic symbols:

SP ! " % & ' ( ) * + , - . / : ; < = > ? _

In the following tables, "numeric" refers to ASCII numerics 0-9, and "alphanumeric" refers to all the allowable characters as specified above. Where numeric characters are indicated in *Content*, if the numeric value is shorter than the length allotted for the element, then the value is right justified and unused positions filled with zeros. Where alphanumeric characters are indicated in Content, if the alphanumeric value is shorter than the length allotted for the element, then the value is left justified and unused positions filled with blanks. The ASCII blank character is code 20_{16}.

Volume Header Label (VOL1):

Element Name	*Bytes*	*Length*	*Content (Description)*
Label Identifier	0-2	3	VOL
Label Number	3	1	1
Volume Identifier	4-9	6	(numeric characters)
Accessibility	10	1	(blank)
Unused	11-36	26	(blanks)
Owner Identifier	37-50	14	(alphanumeric characters)
Unused	51-78	28	(blanks)
Label Standard Version	79	1	1

Example: Library of Congress Volume Header Label (VOL1)

VOL	1	<nnnnnn>	ƀ	<26 ƀ>	LIBROFCONGRESS	<28 ƀ>	1

Note: Library of Congress MARC Distribution Service tapes use unique serial numbers as *Volume Identifiers*. Tapes are also identified in an external label by volume and number as issues in the MARC Distribution Service.

File Header Label (HDR1):

Element Name	*Bytes*	*Length*	*Content (Description)*
Label Identifier	0-2	3	HDR
Label Number	3	1	1
File Identifier	4-20	17	(alphanumeric characters)
File Set Identifier	21-26	6	(numeric characters)
File Section Number	27-30	4	(numeric characters)
File Sequence Number	31-34	4	(numeric characters)
Unused	35-40	6	(blanks)
Creation Date	41-46	6	(numeric characters; ƀyyddd)
Expiration Date	47-52	6	(blanks)
Accessibility	53	1	(blank)
Block Count	54-59	6	000000
System Code	60-72	13	(alphanumeric characters)
Unused	73-79	7	(blanks)

Example: Library of Congress File Header Label (HDR1)

HDR	1	MARC.BOOKSƀƀƀƀƀƀ	<nnnnn>	0001	0001	<6 ƀ>	ƀyyddd

	<6 ƀ>	ƀ	000000	OS370ƀƀƀƀƀƀƀ	<7 ƀ>

Note: The *File Identifier* is different for each Library of Congress MARC Distribution Service. The *File Set Identifier* will be the same as the *Volume Identifier* in VOL1. The *System Code* may vary. The following are representative of those used:

Books (All)	= MARC.BOOKS
Books (English)	= MARC.BOOKS.ENG
Books CJK (Chinese, Japanese, Korean)	= MARC.BOOKS.CJK
Visual Materials	= MARC.VISMAT
Serials	= MARC.SERIALS
Music	= MARC.MUSIC
Name Authorities	= MARC.NAMES
Subject Authorities	= MARC.SUBJECTS
Books (All) [UNIMARC]	= UNIMARC.BOOKS

File Header Label (HDR2):

Element Name	Bytes	Length	Content (Description)
Label Identifier	0-2	3	HDR
Label Number	3	1	2
Record Format	4	1	U
Block Length	5-9	5	02048
Record Length	10-14	5	00000
Unused	15-49	35	(blanks)
Buffer Offset	50-51	2	00
Unused	52-79	28	(blanks)

Example: Library of Congress File Header Label (HDR2)

HDR	2	U	02048	00000	<35 ƀ>	00	<28 ƀ>

End-of-Volume Label (EOV1):

Element Name	Bytes	Length	Content (Description)
Label Identifier	0-2	3	EOV
Label Number	3	1	1
Same as HDR1	4-53	50	(same as HDR1)
Physical Block Count	54-59	6	(numeric characters)
Same as HDR1	60-79	20	(same as HDR1)

Example: Library of Congress End of Volume Label (EOV1)

EOV	1	<same as HDR1>	<nnnnn>	<same as HDR1>

End-of-Volume Label (EOV2):

Element Name	Bytes	Length	Content (Description)
Label Identifier	0-2	3	EOV
Label Number	3	1	2
Same as HDR2	4-79	76	(same as HDR2)

Example: Library of Congress End of Volume Label (EOV2)

EOV	2	<same as HDR2>

End-of-File Label (EOF1):

Element Name	Bytes	Length	Content (Description)
Label Identifier	0-2	3	EOF
Label Number	3	1	1
Same as HDR1	4-53	50	(same as HDR1)
Block Count	54-59	6	(numeric characters)
Same as HDR1	60-79	20	(same as HDR1)

Example: Library of Congress End of File Label (EOF1)

EOF	1	<same as HDR1>	<nnnnnn>	<same as HDR1>

End-of-File Label (EOF2):

Element Name	Bytes	Length	Content (Description)
Label Identifier	0-2	3	EOF
Label Number	3	1	2
Same as HDR2	4-79	76	(same as HDR2)

Example: Library of Congress End of File Label (EOF2)

EOF	2	<same as HDR2>

Tape Record Segmentation

USMARC records, are written to tape using a segmented record technique based on ANSI X3.27. This technique utilizes physical blocks fixed in length at 2048 characters, with records or record segments filling the entire block. Each record, or record segment, is preceded by a five-character **Segment Control Word (SCW)**. The first character position of the SCW is called the Segment Indicator (see below) and contains a value that indicates the content of the segment. The last four character positions of the SCW contain the Segment Length. The Segment Length consists of four ASCII numerics, expressed as a decimal number, giving the length, in bytes, of the record segment plus the length of the SCW. The number is right justified with zero fill.

Segment Indicator (character position 1, ASCII numeric)
0 Record begins and ends in this segment
1 Record begins but does not end in this segment
2 Record neither begins nor ends in this segment
3 Record ends but does not begin in this segment

Segment Length (character positions 2-5, ASCII numerics)
Segment Length includes the 5 characters of the SCW

Record segments may thus span blocks or volumes. However, there may be only one segment of the same record in a block. The segments of a record are written in consecutive order; the segments of other records are not interspersed.

A segment may contain no fewer than six characters; such a segment consists of the SCW and one data character. If at the end of a logical record, less than six positions remain in a block, the block is padded with ASCII blanks and the next logical record begins in the next block. If the last physical block in a file is not completely filled, it is padded to its full length with ASCII blanks following the last data character. For example, if the only segment in the last block in a file is the minimum length of 6 characters, then that block is padded with 2042 ASCII blanks.

While there is no limit to the number of segments comprising one record, USMARC records have a maximum length of 99999 characters. This is the largest number that can be entered in the USMARC Logical Record Length field (Leader, character positions 00-04). Thus, the largest possible USMARC record could be contained in 49 blocks.

Example: Record 1 has logical length of 4231 characters; Record 2 has logical length of 1890 characters; Record 3 has logical length of 1845 characters. Record 3 is the last record.

Block 1:

SCW		DATA
1	2048	2043 char. of Record 1

Block 2:

SCW		DATA
2	2048	2043 char. of Record 1

Block 3:

SCW		DATA	SCW		DATA	PADDING
3	0150	145 char. of Record 1	0	1895	1890 char. of	3 blank

Block 4:

SCW		DATA	PADDING
0	1850	1845 char. of Record 3	198 blank char.

Obsolete Tape Specifications (Pre-1977)

The specifications described below were valid prior to 1977. The primary difference between the obsolete and current tape specifications is that the pre-1977 specifications did not allow for records to be spanned. These specifications became obsolete when the new specifications were adopted by USMARC users at the end of 1977. The tape format and labeling described below are based on those specified in *American National Standard Magnetic Tape Labels for Information Interchange* (ANSI X3.27-1969).

Tape Format

Tapes were available in two formats: nine channel tapes (odd parity) written at 800 bpi and seven channel tapes (odd parity) written at 556 bpi. Tapes contained internal labels written in ASCII. Each label was an 80-byte record, the byte positions of which were numbered, starting with the leftmost byte position, 0 to 79. Each file of records was terminated by a tape mark (character 13_{16} for nine channel, character 17_8 for seven channel).

The total length of a record was given in the first five bytes of each new record. Records were stored in physical units which could contain a minimum of 12 characters up to a maximum of 2048 characters. Each record began at the first of a physical unit. If a record contained less than 2048 characters, then the size of the physical unit matched the size of the record and also contained less than 2048 characters. If the record contained more than 2048 characters, then the first 2048 characters of the record composed the first physical unit, the next 2048 characters the next physical unit, etc. The last physical unit containing the record could be less than 2048 characters in length. However, if the remainder of the record contained less than 12 characters, the physical unit containing this remainder was padded with blanks out to 12 characters.

Tape File Organization

Volume and file organization were as follows:

> Volume Header Label (VOL1)
> File Header Label (HDR1)
> Tape Mark
> File of data records
> Tape Mark
> End of File Label (EOF1)
> Tape Mark
> Tape Mark

Tape Labels

The structure and contents of the internal tape labels were as follows. Where numeric characters are indicated in Content, if the numeric value is shorter than the length allotted for the element, then the value is right justified and unused positions filled with zeros. Where alphanumeric characters are indicated in Content, if the alphanumeric value is shorter than the length allotted for the element, then the value is left justified and unused positions filled with blanks (ASCII character 20_{16}).

Volume Header Label (VOL1)—Nine Channel Tapes:

Element Name	Bytes	Length	Content (Description)
Label Identifier	0-2	3	VOL
Label Number	3	1	1
Volume Serial	4-9	6	(alphanumeric characters)
Accessibility	10	1	(blank)
Unused	11-36	26	(blanks)
Owner Identifier	37-50	14	(alphanumeric characters)
Unused	51-78	28	(blanks)
Label Standard Version	79	1	1

File Header Label (HDR1)—Nine Channel Tapes:

Element Name	Bytes	Length	Content (Description)
Label Identifier	0-2	3	HDR
Label Number	3	1	1
File Identifier	4-20	17	(alphanumeric characters)
File Set Identifier	21-26	6	(alphanumeric characters)
File Section Number	27-30	4	0001
File Sequence Number	31-34	4	0001
Unused	35-40	6	(blanks)
Creation Date	41-46	6	(blank and 5 numeric characters*)
Expiration Date	47-52	6	(blanks)
Accessibility	53	1	(blank)
Block Count	54-59	6	000000
System Code	60-72	13	(alphanumeric characters)
Unused	73-79	7	(blanks)

* The date is formatted *yyddd*, where *yy* = last 2 digits of the year and *ddd* = Julian day.

End of File Label (EOF1)—Nine Channel Tapes:

Element Name	Bytes	Length	Content (Description)
Label Identifier	0-2	3	EOF
Label Number	3	1	1
Same as File Header Label	4-53	50	(same as File Header Label)
Block Count	54-59	6	(numeric characters)
Same as File Header Label	60-79	20	(same as File Header Label)

Tape Labels—Seven Channel Tapes

Seven channel tapes also contained the above labels, but all alphabetic characters were lowercase.

Tape Mark

The tape mark was a special block consisting of a gap of approximately 3.5 inches of tape followed by a single byte containing the character 13_{16} for nine channel tapes and 17_8 for seven channel tapes.

Diskette Specifications

The diskette formatting and labeling specifications used in the distribution of USMARC authority, bibliographic, classification, community information, and holdings records on diskette are described below. These diskette label specifications were provisionally approved by the Library of Congress and the USMARC Advisory Group in November 1990 and apply to internal diskette labels only.

Microcomputer diskette volume and file labels, like tape labels, communicate information from the originating system to the receiving system. The volume and file labels identify and characterize the diskette(s), the transaction, and the information contained on the microcomputer diskette(s). The volume and file labels provide an eye-readable display of identifying information and also enable machine processing of the information.

Diskette Format

A USMARC microcomputer diskette for information interchange is a magnetic diskette (e.g., 5.25 inch floppy or 3.5 inch microdisc) that contains label files and at least one file of MARC records.

Diskette File Organization

Files may be organized for a transaction in one of three ways: 1) single volume, single file; 2) single volume, multiple files; and 3) multiple volumes, multiple files. (Each single diskette constitutes one volume.) Record blocking is *not* used and individual records do not span files or volumes. Files do not span volumes. Large logical files of records can be segmented into multiple physical files on separate volumes. The following configurations may be used. **NOTE:** The names in parentheses are required filenames. The portions in italics are sequential numbers determined by the originator of the volume(s)/file(s).

Single volume, Single file

Volume Label File (VOL.*nnn*)
File Label File (FIL.*nnn*)
Bibliographic File

Single volume, Multiple files

Volume Label File (VOL.*nnn*)
File Label File (FIL.*nnn*)
Bibliographic File
File Label File (FIL.*nnn*)
Bibliographic File

Multiple volumes, Multiple files

Volume A
Volume Label File (VOL.*nnn*)
File Label File (FIL.*nnn*)
Bibliographic File
File Label File (FIL.*nnn*)
Bibliographic File

Volume B
Volume Label File (VOL.*nnn*)
File Label File (FIL.*nnn*)
Bibliographic File
File Label File (FIL.*nnn*)
Bibliographic File

Diskette Label Files

USMARC Microcomputer diskettes contain label files that identify and characterize the volume(s) and the file(s) of USMARC records. The label files are used to transfer non-MARC information between an originating system and a receiving system. The label files are written using only ASCII Latin characters. A **volume label** file is required for each new physical volume (i.e., each diskette). A **file label** file is required for each named file of USMARC records. Diskettes should also bear an external eye-readable label which lists the Originating System ID (ORS), the Volume ID (VID), and the Date Volume(s) Compiled (DAT).

Diskette File Names

File names for label files must accommodate dissimilar operating systems, but primarily PC-DOS, MS-DOS, APPLE-DOS and Macintosh environments. While certain operating systems have more flexible naming conventions than others, label files are named according to DOS filename conventions that specify filenames of 1-to-8 characters and a 1-to-3 character extension. Alphabetic characters in filenames and extensions shall be in uppercase.

Volume label files are named "VOL.*nnn*" (*nnn* are numerics designating the volumes, e.g., VOL.001, VOL.002). The 3-digit numeric extensions in the filename are assigned in a sequential order, and the highest number in the extension will equal the total number of volumes in a transaction.

File label files are named "FIL.*nnn*" (*nnn* are numerics designating the files, e.g., FIL.001).

Record files are named according to DOS naming conventions that allow names of 1-8 characters in length, a 1-3 character extension, etc. (e.g., SERMARC.*nnn*). The 3-digit numeric filename extension of the bibliographic file will match the 3-digit numeric filename extension of the file label with which it is associated.

Structure

A label file consists of a sequence of fields. Fields have a maximum length of 80 characters. Each field in a label file begins with a three-character tag identifying the field. The tag is followed by two blanks (ASCII character 20_{16}). The field's data content follows the two blanks. Each field ends with a number sign "#" (ASCII character 23_{16}) and a carriage return (ASCII character $0D_{16}$) or carriage return/line feed *(ASCII characters $0D_{16}$ $0A_{16}$)*, dependent on operating systems and subject to the agreement between originating and receiving systems. The 80 character maximum length of the field includes the three character tag, the two blanks, the data content, the number sign, and the carriage return or carriage return/line feed. This results in a text string that is easily displayed on a monitor or printed out.

Certain fields in the label files are specified as mandatory and must be present in each label file. In these fields, data content or one fill character—the vertical bar (| - ASCII character $7C_{16}$), must be supplied. Mandatory or optional characteristics of the fields are noted below.

Several of the fields are repeatable when either of the following two conditions exist: 1) the data content exceeds the space available in the field (73 characters between the blank space and number sign); or, 2) for eye readability, the sections of the data are moved to a new line. In each case, the three-character tag and two blank spaces are repeated.

Diskette Volume Labels – Tags/Fields

The following order of the fields in the volume label is mandatory whether or not all fields are present.

Tag	Element Name	Description	Mandatory /Optional	Repeatable
ORS	Originating System ID	Alphanumeric	M	NR
RCS	Receiving System ID	Alphanumeric	O	R
DAT	Date Volume(s) Compiled	YYYYMMDD	M	NR
DES	Description of Records	Alphanumeric	O	R
TRN	Transaction ID	Alphanumeric	O	NR
VID	Volume ID	Numeric	M	NR
VTR	No. of Vols. in Transaction	Numeric	M*	NR
BFV	Bibl. Files in Volume	Numeric	M	NR
BFT	Bibl. Files in Transaction	Numeric	O	NR
PON	Purchase Order Number(s)	Alphanumeric	O	R
INV	Invoice No(s). in Transaction	Alphanumeric	O	R
CSN	Transaction Bill-To ID	Alphanumeric	O	NR
LOC	Location(s)	Alphanumeric	O	R
NOT	Note(s)	Alphanumeric	O	R

*Field VTR is only mandatory on the final volume of a transaction.

ORS (Originating System ID): Mandatory. Not Repeatable. The name of the system that compiled the files of records and produced the volume(s) in the transaction. Alphanumeric.

RCS (Receiving System ID): Optional. Repeatable. Number(s) and/or name(s) of the receiving system(s) (e.g., library, processing center, school, collection, agency, or office) of the records in this transaction. The number/name can be assigned by the system listed in the field ORS, chosen by the system listed in this field, or a designated standard number, i.e., SAN. Multiple names are separated by two blank spaces followed by a backslash (\ - ASCII character $5C_{16}$). Alphanumeric.

DAT (Date Volume(s) Compiled): Mandatory. Not Repeatable. This is the date when the originating system completed the compilation of bibliographic records on the volume(s) in this transaction. This is not the date of the creation of the particular bibliographic records contained in the bibliographic files. This field is recorded according to *Representation for Calendar Date and Ordinal Date for Information Interchange* (ANSI X3.30). The date requires 8 numeric characters in the pattern *yyyymmdd* (4 for the year, 2 for the month, and 2 for the day; right justified and zero filled).

DES (Description of Records): Optional. Repeatable. A descriptions of the records contained on the volume or the application(s) for which the records are intended to be used (e.g., test records, cataloging, union list, USMARC Holdings, etc.) Alphanumeric.

TRN (Transaction ID): Optional. Not Repeatable. Identifier that identifies a volume or set of volumes transferred in one operation. Alphanumeric.

VID (Volume ID): Mandatory. Not Repeatable. Numeric identifier of the volume. Three numeric characters, right justified and zero filled.

VTR (Number of Volumes in Transaction): Mandatory on Final Volume of Transaction Only; Optional on Other Volumes. Not Repeatable. The total number of volumes in this transaction. Three numeric characters, right justified and zero filled.

BFV (Bibliographic Files on Volume): Mandatory. Not Repeatable. The total number of bibliographic files on the volume. Three numeric characters, right justified and zero filled.

BFT (Bibliographic Files in Transaction): Optional. Not Repeatable. The total number of bibliographic files on all the diskettes in this transaction. Three numeric characters, right justified and zero filled.

PON (Purchase Order Number(s)): Optional. Repeatable. The purchase orders number(s) covered by the transaction. Alphanumeric.

INV (Invoice Number(s) in Transaction): Optional. Repeatable. This includes all invoice numbers for all files in this transaction. Alphanumeric.

CSN (Transaction Bill-To ID): Optional. Not Repeatable. Number and/or name of the agency/institution which is billed for the transaction. The number/name can be assigned by the system listed in the field ORS, chosen by the system listed in this field, or a designated standard number, i.e., SAN. Alphanumeric.

LOC (Location(s)): Optional. Repeatable. This field lists the locations related to the records in the bibliographic files of the transaction. Multiple locations are separated by two blank spaces followed by a backslash (\ - ASCII character $5C_{16}$). NUC or other codes can be used to designate locations. Alphanumeric.

NOT (Note(s)): Optional. Repeatable. This field is available for textual information, messages, etc. Alphanumeric.

Example of volume label: File name "VOL.001" (Filename extension corresponds to the VID)

```
ORSbb<originating system identification>#
RCSbbUniversity of Michigan Library Processing Center#
DATbb19900322#
DESbbCataloging#
TRNbb03201990NAR#
VIDbb001#
VTRbb022#
BFVbb002#
BFTbb893#
PONbb12311989UML#
INVbb1211990CDS#
CSNbbUniversity of Michigan Financial Office#
LOCbbLaw Library  \Medical Library  \Engineering Library#
NOTbbContact B. Smith, (202) 707-1111, if you have questions.#
```

Diskette File Labels – Tags/Fields

The following order of the fields in the file label is mandatory whether or not all fields are present.

Tag	Element Name	Description	Mandatory /Optional	Repeatable
VID	Volume Number ID	Numeric	O	NR
FID	File ID	Alphanumeric	M	NR
DES	Description of Records	Alphanumeric	O	R
RBF	Records in Bibl. File	Numeric	M	NR
INV	Invoice Number(s) Covering Records in File	Alphanumeric	O	R
LOC	Location(s)	Alphanumeric	O	R
NOT	Note(s)	Alphanumeric	O	R

VID (Volume ID): Optional. Not Repeatable. Numeric identifier of the volume. Three numeric characters, right justified and zero filled.

FID (File ID): Mandatory. Not Repeatable. Identifier that gives the name and/or number of the file containing the records. Alphanumeric.

DES (Description of Records): Optional. Repeatable. Indicates the application(s) for which the records are intended to be used (e.g., cataloging, union list, test records, USMARC Holdings, etc.) Alphanumeric.

RBF (Number of Records in Bibliographic File): Mandatory. Not Repeatable. The total number of records contained in the file. Seven numeric characters, right justified and zero filled.

INV (Invoice Number(s) Covering the Records in Bibliographic File): Optional. Repeatable. This includes all invoice numbers for all records in the bibliographic file. Alphanumeric.

LOC (Locations): Optional. Repeatable. This field lists the locations related to the records in the file. Multiple locations are separated by two blanks followed by a backslash (\ - ASCII character $5C_{16}$). USMARC or other codes can be used to designate locations. Alphanumeric.

NOT (Note(s)): Optional. Repeatable. This field is available for textual information, messages, etc. Alphanumeric.

Example of file label: File name: "FIL.002" (Filename extension corresponds to the FID)

```
VIDbb001#
FIDbb002#
DESbbUnion Catalog Records#
RBFbb0000258#
INVbb1211990CDS#
LOCbbUMML#
NOTbbRecords are in LCCN order per your request#
```

Diskette Directory Display

The USMARC diskette volume and file label files are designed to allow the determination of the content of a diskette by listing its directory using the DOS "dir" command (or similar command in other system environments). Below is an example of the directory listing for a typical diskette containing files of USMARC records. In this example, the diskette contains three files of bibliographic records.

```
A:>  dir

Volume in drive A is 001
Directory of A:\

VOL.001
FIL.001
BOOKMARC.001
FIL.002
SERMARC.002
FIL.003
VMMARC.003
```

Since the data and files on microcomputer diskettes are usually accessed in random order, the sequence of the various files listed in the directory does not matter. The example above has ordered the files so as to show the correspondence between the file label files and the bibliographic files.

Electronic File Transfer Specifications

The specifications for transfering files of USMARC records electronically assume the use of a standard protocol. The File Transfer Protocol (FTP) is the most generally used. FTP can be used in place of a physical exchange medium to move USMARC authority, bibliographic, classification, community information, and holdings records from a storage device in an originating system to a receiving system. These electronic file transfer specifications were approved by the Library of Congress and the USMARC Advisory Group in June 1993.

The labels used with electronic file transfer, like tape and diskette volume and file labels, communicate information from the originating system to the receiving system. The labels identify and characterize the transaction and the information contained in the data that is being transferred electronically. The labels will make possible an eye-readable display of the identifying information and also enable machine processing of the information.

Electronic Transfer File Organization

Each file of USMARC records should accompany a corresponding label file containing bibliographic file and volume information. The label and record file pair can be transferred separately or they can be compressed (archived) into a single file for transfer by the originating system. It is then up to the receiving system to decompress (restore) the label and record file(s). The concept of physical *volumes* does not apply to electronic transfers as it does to exchange using dismountable physical media, but the identification of volumes may be particularly useful with groups of files compressed for transfer into a single file. Record blocking is *not* used and individual records do not span files or transfers. Large logical files of records can be segmented into multiple physical files during separate transfers. The following configurations may be used.

Uncompressed transfer	**Compressed transfer**
Label File	Compressed File
Bibliographic File	Label File 1
	Bibliographic File 1
	Label File *n*
	Bibliographic File *n*

Electronic Transfer Label Files

A file of *USMARC* records is transferred electronically following a label file that identifies and characterizes the file of USMARC records, and optionally, the volume to which it belongs. **NOTE:** volume information is *not* transmitted in a separate file as is done with tape and diskette. The label file is used to transfer non-MARC information between an originating system and a receiving system. The label file is written using only ASCII Latin characters. A **label file** is required for each file of USMARC records transmitted.

Electronic Transfer File Names

These USMARC specifications do not mandate the length or style of file names due to differences between operating systems. Exchange partners should agree upon file naming conventions prior to transferring USMARC records electronically.

Structure

A label file consists of a sequence of fixed-length and variable fields. The order of fields should be the same as the list below. The length of fixed-length fields is specified in the descriptions of those fields. Variable length fields have no maximum length. Each field in a label file begins with a three-character tag followed by two blanks (ASCII character 20_{16}). The field's data content follows the two blanks. Each field ends with an end-of-field marker (ASCII control character $1E_{16}$) immediately following the data in the field.

Certain fields in the label files are specified as mandatory and must be present in each label file. In these fields, data content or one fill character—the vertical bar (| - ASCII character $7C_{16}$), must be supplied. Mandatory or optional characteristics of the fields are also noted below. Several of the fields are repeatable.

Electronic Transfer File (and Volume) Labels—Tags/Fields

The following order of the fields in the file label is mandatory whether or not all fields are present.

Tag	Element Name	Description	Mandatory /Optional	Fixed/ Variable	Repeatable
DAT	Date compiled	YYYYMMDDHHMMSS.F	M	F	NR
RBF	Number of records	Numeric	M	V	NR
DSN	Data Set Name	Alphanumeric	M	V	NR
ORS	Originating system ID	Alphanumeric	M	V	NR
DTS	Date sent	YYYYMMDDHHMMSS.F	O	F	NR
DTR	Dates of records	YYYYMMDDYYYYMMDD	O	F	NR
FOR	Format	Alphanumeric	O	F	NR
DES	Description	Alphanumeric	O	V	R
VOL	Volume	Alphanumeric	O	V	R
ISS	Issue	Alphanumeric	O	V	R
REP	Reply to	Alphanumeric	O	V	R
NOT	Note	Alphanumeric	O	V	R

DAT (Date compiled): Mandatory; Fixed length; Not repeatable. This is the date the originating system completed the compilation of the file of records. This is not the date of the creation of the records contained in the bibliographic file. The field is recorded according to *Representation for Calendar Date and Ordinal Date for Information Interchange* (ANSI X3.30) and *Representations of Local Time of the Day for Information Interchange* (ANSI X3.43). The date requires 8 numeric characters in the pattern *yyyymmdd* (4 for the year, 2 for the month, and 2 for the day; right justified and zero filled). The time requires 8 numeric characters in the pattern **hhmmss.f** (2 for the hour, 2 for the minute, 2 for the second, and 2 for a decimal fraction of the second, including the decimal point). The 24-hour clock is used.

RBF (Number of records in file): Mandatory; Variable length; Non-repeatable. This element includes the number of logical records contained in the file of USMARC records.

DSN (Data Set Name): Mandatory; Variable length; Not repeatable. The filename of the file of USMARC records (which is sent separately) for which this is a file label.

ORS (Originating system ID): Mandatory; Variable length; Not repeatable. The name of the system that compiled the files of records. This could be a symbol (e.g., OCLC or NUC) or text.

DTS (Date sent): Optional; Fixed length; Not repeatable. This is the date of transmission of the file of USMARC records. The field is recorded according to *Representation for Calendar Date and Ordinal Date for Information Interchange* (ANSI X3.30) and *Representations of Local Time of the Day for Information Interchange* (ANSI X3.43). The date requires 8 numeric characters in the pattern *yyyymmdd* (4 for the year, 2 for the month, and 2 for the day; right justified and zero filled). The time requires 8 numeric characters in the pattern **hhmmss.f** (2 for the hour, 2 for the minute, 2 for the second, and 2 for a decimal fraction of the second, including the decimal point). The 24-hour clock is used.

DTR (Dates of records): Optional; Fixed length; Not repeatable. This includes inclusive dates of last transaction of the records in the file, i.e. the first and last date recorded in the 005 fields of the file of records. The field is recorded according to *Representation for Calendar Date and Ordinal Date for Information Interchange* (ANSI X3.30). The date requires 16 numeric characters in the pattern *yyyymmddyyymmdd* (4 for the year, 2 for the month, and 2 for the day for each date; right justified and zero filled).

FOR (Format): Optional; Fixed length; Not repeatable. This element designates the format of the records, generally M for MARC. Other codes may be defined as needed (e.g., Z for Z39.2 for copyright records.

DES (Description of records): Optional; Variable length; Repeatable. This element describes the records. The data could be coded or describe a product name. (For example, OCLC uses B for Bibliographic describing a data type; CDS may use a product name, such as MDS-Books All.)

VOL (Volume): Optional; Variable length; Repeatable. This may be used if it is desirable to assign a volume number when distribution of records is by subscription. Each file within a subscription year may be given a volume and issue number.

ISS (Issue): Optional; Variable length; Repeatable. This may be used if it is desirable to assign a volume and issue number when distribution of records is by subscription. Each file within a subscription year may be given a volume and issue number. It may be combined with Volume (e.g., V1402).

REP (Reply to): Optional; Variable length; Repeatable. This field contains an address given as a contact for problems/questions in transmission. It may include an Internet or postal address.

NOT (Note): Optional; Variable length; Repeatable. This field contains textual information or messages about the file.

Electronic Transfer of USMARC Label and Record Files

Each file is transferred electronically as a separate operation. If no compression is involved, a label file should be transferred preceding the USMARC record file to which it relates. If label and record files have been compressed, the transfer of all data can occur as a single operation to the receiving system. In this case, the receiving system must process the compressed file to restore the label and record file(s) as separate files.

Example of an electronic file transfer label file: (" < EOF > " = end-of-field character)

DATƀƀ19940311141236.0 < EOF >
RBFƀƀ1564 < EOF >
DSNƀƀLOC.NAMES.DIST.DATA.D940311 < EOF >
ORSƀƀDLC < EOF >
DTSƀƀ19940312083152.0 < EOF >
DTRƀƀ1994010119940230 < EOF >
FORƀƀM < EOF >
DESƀƀMDS-Books All < EOF >
VOLƀƀV21 < EOF >
ISSƀƀIXX < EOF >